ARTS and CRAFTS for ALL SEASONS

www.themailbox.com

The Education Center®

Arts and Crafts for All Seasons
Preschool / kindergarten: TEC926

Created for The Education Center, Inc., by
Two-Can Publishing Ltd., 346 Old Street,
London EC1V 9RB, U.K.

Craft authors
Diane James
Ivan Bulloch
Melanie Williams
Claire Watts

Illustrators
Kelly Dooley
Jo Moore
Claire Boyce
Michael Evans
Sonia Canals

www.themailbox.com

Printed in the United States
10 9 8 7

Contents

Art Tips

About This Book

● For each project, materials are listed in quantities for one child. Simply multiply the quantities given by the number of children in your class to work out your exact requirements.

● To save time and avoid waste, most projects use standard paper sizes, or can be easily cut from them. All other materials are standard sizes unless stated. The glue used is ordinary white school glue.

● A section called "Class Preparations" is included for projects which require simple pre-lesson preparations. Teachers' materials or equipment, such as a hole puncher or a stapler, are included here if needed.

● Step-by-step directions guide you through every stage of the project. An ⓗ symbol indicates that the children may need particular help at this step. The ⓣ symbol indicates that you will need to carry out the step yourself as it might involve cutting, tying, or displaying artwork.

● Some projects include patterns to duplicate. The easiest method of copying onto tagboard or construction paper is to use a photocopier. Alternatively, trace a pattern, cut out the shape, and use it as a template to trace the shape onto individual sheets of paper.

● All the projects are simple and easy to make, but it's a good idea to try them out first: you'll understand them fully and have a sample to show the class.

Collecting Materials

● At the start of the year, send children home with a duplicated letter requesting scrap materials. Write your own or copy the letter on page 6. Check the items you need, add others not on the list, and sign your name. Repeat the letter whenever supplies are running low or you need a specific item.

● When requesting specific items, such as family photographs for Family Tree (page 11), write the date that the item is needed, give the dimensions if important, and remember to give out the letter well in advance.

● For large quantities of one item, such as pizza boxes for Pick Up A Pizza (page 141), put up a "Wanted" notice on your classroom door. Staff and other pupils may be able to help by recycling used packaging.

● Think ahead—have children bring in used cards and gift wrap after Christmas, Easter, and other celebrations. You may not need them right away, but they're sure to come in handy in the future.

● Ask parents to donate old shirts. Have the children put them on backward, then button them up and roll back the sleeves. Now you have an art smock that will protect clothes against paint and glue.

● Encourage your youngsters to take care of the environment. Warn them against picking wild flowers or taking live bark, twigs, and leaves from trees. Ask them to gather natural materials by searching on the ground for fallen foliage.

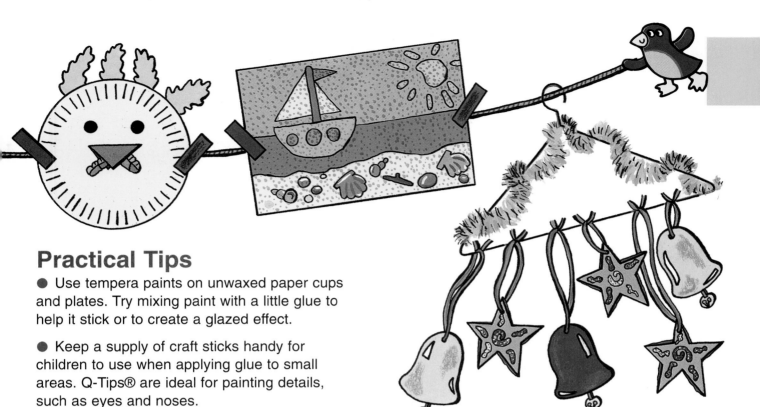

Practical Tips

● Use tempera paints on unwaxed paper cups and plates. Try mixing paint with a little glue to help it stick or to create a glazed effect.

● Keep a supply of craft sticks handy for children to use when applying glue to small areas. Q-Tips® are ideal for painting details, such as eyes and noses.

● For collages, try tearing paper instead of cutting. It's a great time-saver and gives a different effect. Add a touch of brightness with colored cellophane or aluminum-foil scraps.

● Supervise children closely when using small, edible items. Be sure to check for allergies before starting projects that use nuts. When gluing candies, ensure that the children do not eat any that may have glue on them. Provide extra candies just for eating.

● When painting hands, feet etc. to make prints, add a little liquid detergent to the paint. It will wash off more easily.

Displaying Craft Projects

● Hang a clothesline across your classroom and use clothespins for hanging artwork. It's a useful way to dry paintings, too.

● Display long artwork, such as the Pretzel Garland (page 42), as a bulletin-board trim or as a decoration around the edges of the chalkboard.

● Designate a shelf or windowsill for displaying 3-D projects. Or hang several pieces of work as a mobile. Decorate a wire coat hanger and hang artwork from the bottom wire using ribbons in different colors and lengths.

Techniques and Recipes

● **Accordion-folding**
This technique is great for greetings cards and pop-up features. Fold a small flap upward at one end of a piece of paper. Turn the paper over and fold the flap backward, to the same width as before. Continue to the end of the paper.

● **Perfect Circles**
When an activity requires a large circle template, tie a piece of string to a pin. Cut the string to the radius of the circle you need and tie a pencil to the end. Push the pin into the center of a sheet of paper and hold upright. Then, keep the string taut and the pencil held upright as you draw the circle.

● **Cornstarch Clay**
This makes a cheap alternative to self-hardening modeling clay. In a saucepan, combine one cup of cornstarch, two cups of baking soda, and one cup plus one tablespoon of water. Cook over a medium heat until thick. When cool, knead well. Powdered tempera paint can be added to the clay before it cools to color it, or the clay can be painted when it has hardened.

Dear Parent

Can you help us collect some art supplies? Most of these items are things you would usually throw away. Please clean them out, save them up, and send them to school with your child.

We need the items checked below:

- ❑ egg cartons
- ❑ cardboard cartons
- ❑ glass jars
- ❑ liquid detergent bottles
- ❑ plastic bottles
- ❑ yogurt containers
- ❑ plastic drinking straws
- ❑ cardboard tubes
- ❑ aluminum foil
- ❑ Styrofoam® dishes
- ❑ paper cups
- ❑ paper plates

- ❑ aluminum foil dishes
- ❑ Styrofoam® packing material
- ❑ bubble wrap
- ❑ fabric scraps
- ❑ yarn
- ❑ ribbon
- ❑ buttons
- ❑ newspapers
- ❑ magazines and catalogs
- ❑ gift wrap
- ❑ old greetings cards
- ❑ sponges
- ❑ clothespins

Others

- ❑ _____
- ❑ _____
- ❑ _____

Thank you!

fall

Bottle-Top Crop

● ●

Materials For Each Child:
1 sheet of 9" x 12" construction paper
green construction-paper scraps
1 plastic soda-bottle top
brown and red tempera paints
   in shallow dishes
paintbrushes
glue

Class Preparations:
Collect a class supply of
soda-bottle tops.

Directions:
1. Paint a brown tree trunk and branches
on the sheet of paper.
2. Dip the top surface of the bottle top in
red paint, then press it down on a branch to
represent an apple.
3. Keep printing until the tree is full of apples.
Allow to dry.
4. Glue on torn green construction-paper
leaves to fill in the spaces on the tree.

Basket Of Apples

● ●

Materials For Each Child:
1/6 sheet of 12" x 18" construction paper
1/4 apple
brown, red, and green tempera paints
   in shallow dishes
brown and black markers

Class Preparations:
For each child, cut a 6" x 6" piece of
construction paper. Cut apples into quarters.

Directions:
1. Dip a quarter apple in brown paint. Press
down on the paper to make a basket print.
2. Dip your finger in red paint and print
some red apples above the basket shape.
3. Print some green apples the same way.
Allow to dry.
4. Use the markers to draw a handle on
the basket and to add stalks to the apples.

Oodles Of Doodles

Materials For Each Child:
6 sheets of 9" x 12" drawing paper
colored markers or construction-paper scraps
1 piece of string or ribbon, about 20" in length
glue

Class Preparations:
For each child, stack six sheets of paper together. Use a hole puncher to punch holes in the left-hand side, as shown.

Directions:
1. Thread string or ribbon through the holes to join the sheets of paper together. ⒣
2. Tie the ends of the string or ribbon in a bow. ⓣ
3. Write your name on the front of your booklet. ⒣
4. Decorate the cover with markers, or glue on paper scraps.
5. Fill your booklet with oodles of doodles!

What A Funny Face!

Materials For Each Child:
1 sheet of 9" x 12" construction paper in a skin tone
magazines to share
short lengths of yarn (optional)
pencil and glue

Class Preparations:
Have your youngsters bring in magazines. Gather a class supply of construction paper in a variety of skin tones.

Directions:
1. Tear pictures of facial features from several different magazines.
2. Draw a simple face outline on a sheet of construction paper.
3. Glue your torn-out features inside the outline to create a wildly wacky face!
4. If desired, glue on yarn pieces for hair.

9

Sharing gifts is a great way for children to make friends at the beginning of the school year.

Friendship Bracelet

Materials For Each Child:
1 pipe cleaner
plastic straws of various colors,
   cut into sections

Class Preparations:
Cut the straws into small sections so that each child has enough pieces to complete the bracelet. Make a small loop at one end of each pipe cleaner so the straw pieces will stay on when the children thread them.

Directions:
1. Thread the pieces of straw onto a pipe cleaner, alternating colors to make a pattern.
2. When the pipe cleaner is full, twist the two ends together to form a bracelet. (H)

Dip-And-Dye Surprise!

Materials For Each Child:
4 different-colored food colorings
   in small dishes, to share
1 paper towel
1 piece of ribbon, 8" in length
small candies

Class Preparations:
Fill each dish with a different color of food coloring and water. Cut an 8" length of ribbon for each child.

Directions:
1. Fold a paper towel in half, then in half again. (H)
2. Dip each corner of the folded paper towel into a different color dye.
3. Unfold the paper towel and let it dry.
4. Put a few small candies in the center of the towel and gather the towel's edges together to make a pouch. (H)
5. Tie a ribbon around the neck of the pouch. (T)

A Work Of Art!

Materials For Each Child:
a small picture the child has created
4 flexible straws in 1"–2" lengths
glue

Class Preparations:
Cut off the flexible portions from a supply
of straws so that each child has four to
use as corners. Then cut the remainder
of the straws into 1"–2" lengths so children
have an assortment of sizes to work with.

Directions:
1. Spread glue around the edge of your picture.
2. Position a flexible straw piece at each corner
of the picture.
3. Fill in the space along the sides of your
picture with short pieces of straw.

Family Tree

Materials For Each Child:
1 sheet of 9" x 12" construction paper
red crepe-paper circles
photos of the child's family members
brown and green tempera paints in
    large, flat containers
glue

Class Preparations:
Use a jar lid 2"–3" in diameter as a template to
cut circles of crepe paper. Each child needs a
circle for each member of his family and for
himself. Pour the paints into flat containers.

Directions:
1. To make the tree, dip the palm of your hand
and the inside of your arm in the brown paint
and make a print on the paper. Allow to dry for
about half an hour.
2. Cut out the photos to fit on the red circles. 🇹
3. Glue the photos on the red circles.
4. Glue the red circles onto the tree's branches.
5. Dip your finger in green paint and use it to
print leaves all over the tree.

11

Springy Star Pencil Topper

Materials For Each Child:
2 tagboard star cutouts
1 pipe cleaner
glitter, pencil and glue

Class Preparations:
For each child, use the
pattern below to cut two slit-and-slot
star pieces from colored tagboard.
Have tape ready.

Directions:
1. Make a glue pattern on one side of
each star and sprinkle with glitter.
2. Allow to dry; then do the same on the
other side.
3. Slot the stars together, as shown.
4. Wrap the pipe cleaner around the pencil to
make a coil. Straighten out a short length at one
end and tape this to the star. ⊕
5. Gently pull down
the pencil so a few
coils spring off
the end.

12

Why not take your students on a nature walk to collect fallen leaves? Compare different colors and shapes.

Lots Of Leaves

Materials For Each Child:
1 sheet of 9" x 12" pastel
   construction paper
2 leaves
1 safety pin
green and brown construction paper, to share
fall-colored tempera paints in shallow dishes

Class Preparations:
For this group and individual project, make a class collection of leaves. Pour thick paints in fall colors into individual shallow dishes.
Have tape and
scissors ready.

Directions:
1. Choose two leaves to dip in paint.
2. Place the veined side of each leaf down in a dish of paint, press gently, and carefully lift. ⓗ
3. Press the leaves down evenly onto pastel paper. Remove gently; then allow prints to dry.
4. Write your name and cut around the prints. One print is for a class tree, the other for a pin. ⓣ
5. Tape one leaf print to a safety pin and wear it so that all your new classmates get to know your name. ⓣ
6. Tear strips of green and brown paper in bark shapes and tape these pieces on the classroom wall in overlapping layers, as shown. ⓗ
7. Arrange and attach all the remaining leaf prints to create a class tree. ⓗ

fall

Use with Fancy Foliage and
Lively Leaves on page 15.

Use with Sunflower
on page 18.

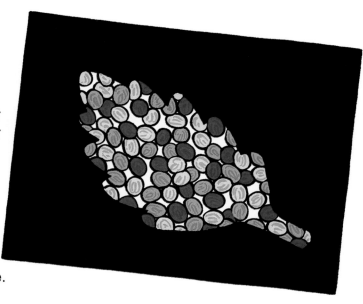

Fancy Foliage

Materials For Each Child:
1 sheet of 9" x 12" black construction paper
1 sheet of 9" x 12" white construction paper
1 leaf template, to share
red, yellow, and green tempera paints
  in shallow dishes
pencil and glue

Class Preparations:
Use the leaf pattern on the opposite page
to create templates for the children to share.
Have scissors ready.

Directions:
1. Use the template to trace a leaf in the center
of the black paper.
2. Cut out the leaf shape so that a black
frame remains. **T**
3. Fingerpaint a white sheet of paper with red,
yellow, and green paints. Allow to dry.
4. Glue the leaf-shaped frame on top of the
painted sheet. **H**

Lively Leaves

Materials For Each Child:
1 leaf cutout made from a coffee filter
1 Styrofoam® meat tray
orange, yellow, and red food coloring
eye drop dispensers, to share and glue

Class Preparations:
For this group project, have your children find
a fallen branch that is an interesting shape. Fill
a container with gravel or sand. For each child,
use the pattern on the opposite page to cut out
a leaf shape from a coffee filter.

Directions:
1. Use an eye drop dispenser to place a few
drops of different-colored food colorings on
a Styrofoam® tray. Add a few drops of water.
2. Lay a leaf cutout on the tray. Set aside
to dry.
3. Fold the tab of each cutout over a different
section of the branch and glue it in place. **H**
4. Insert the branch into a container filled with
sand or gravel. **T**

Explain that a full, harvest moon shines specially bright. Farmers can even harvest their crops by its light.

Harvest Moon
• •

Materials For Each Child:
¼ sheet of 9" x 12" black construction paper
1 black construction-paper circle, 3" in diameter
1 yellow construction-paper circle, 3" in diameter
star stickers
glue and Sticky Tac®

Class Preparations:
For each child, cut a piece of 4½" x 6" black construction paper. Use a jar lid to make 3" yellow circles and 3" black circles. Describe how the moon seems to change during the year.

Directions:
1. Glue a yellow circle on top of a black circle.
2. Fold a small portion of the black side of your circle over the yellow side to form a flap. 🅗
3. Now glue the larger portion of your circle on a sheet of black paper.
4. Fold the flap flat against the paper to show a harvest moon or fold it over the circle to show a crescent moon!
5. Secure the flap with Sticky Tac®. Then complete the moon picture with star stickers.

Big Autumn Sun
• •

Materials For Each Child:
1 sheet of 9" x 12" yellow posterboard
dried grasses, flowers, and corn husks
orange and brown tempera paints
paintbrushes and glue

Class Preparations:
Help the class to collect grasses and flowers outside. Spread them out on newspaper to dry. Or purchase dried flowers and corn husks.

Directions:
1. Paint the bottom half of the yellow posterboard brown.
2. Paint an orange sun in the top half of the posterboard. Allow to dry.
3. Arrange and glue dried grasses, flowers, and corn husks, to the area painted brown.

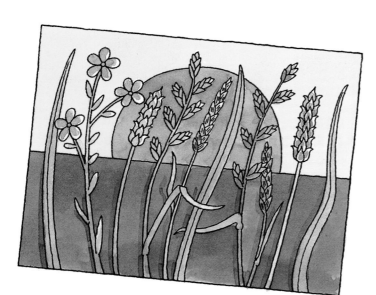

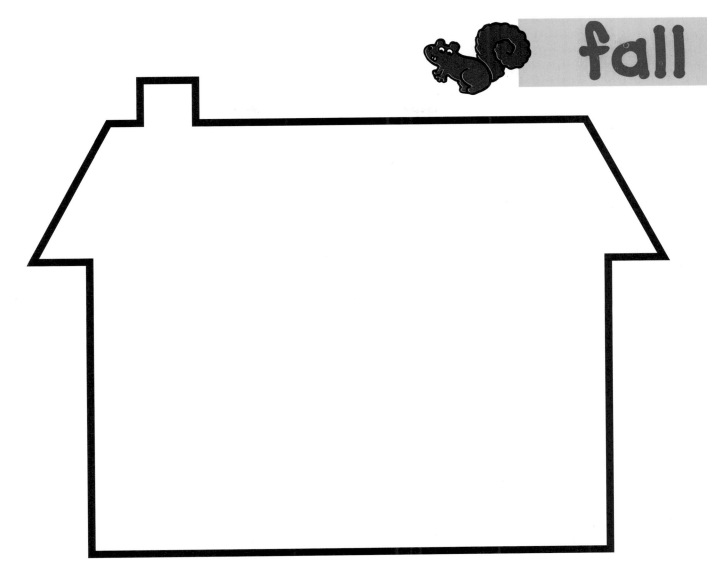

Fields Of Grain

Materials For Each Child:
1 colored construction-paper house cutout
1 sheet of 12" x 18" tagboard
materials with different textures such as corn,
    rice, seeds, and grass clippings
tempera paints
paintbrushes, pencil, and glue

Class Preparations:
For each child, use the pattern on this page to
cut out a house from colored construction paper.

Directions:
1. Draw lines from corner to corner of the
tagboard to separate the background into
different fields. ⊕

2. Spread glue on each section in turn, and fill
in each of the fields with a different texture, such
as rice, seeds, and grass.
3. Paint a roof, door, and windows on the house
cutout and glue on the middle of the tagboard.

fall

Sunflower

. . . .

Materials For Each Child:
8 yellow construction-paper petal cutouts
1 paper plate, 7" in diameter
1 cork
black tempera paint in a shallow dish
yellow tempera paint and paintbrush
glue

Class Preparations:
Use the pattern on page 14 to cut about eight yellow construction-paper petals for each child.

Directions:
1. Paint the paper plate yellow. Allow to dry.
2. Dip the end of a cork in black paint and press down in the center of the plate. Keep printing until you have covered most of the plate's center.
3. Glue the petal cutouts around the rim of the plate.

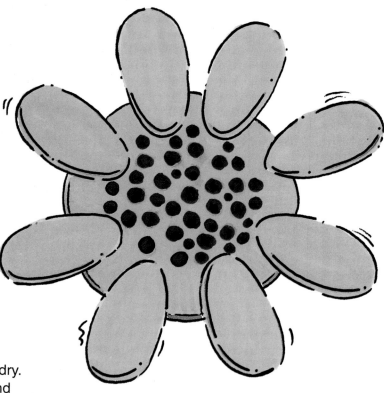

Veggie Beast

. . . .

Materials For Each Child:
1 sheet of 9" x 12" construction paper
1/2 small cabbage
a variety of other vegetable halves (broccoli, carrot, mushroom, potato, etc.), to share
thick tempera paints in shallow pans

Class Preparations:
Cut a cabbage and other vegetables in half. Pour a different color of paint into each shallow pan. Arrange several different vegetable halves beside each pan of paint.

Directions:
1. Dip a cabbage half in the paint, then press it firmly on your paper to make a face print.
2. Now use the other vegetables to add facial features and hair to your veggie monster.

18

Shoo!

· · · · · · · · ·

Materials For Each Child:
1 fabric square, 2" x 2"
1 colored tagboard circle, 1½" in diameter
1 plastic cup
2 craft sticks
modeling clay and raffia
black marker and glue

Class Preparations:
For each child, cut a square of fabric, and use a bottle top to trace and cut a circle from tagboard.

Directions:
1. Put a piece of clay in the bottom of your cup.
2. Glue the craft sticks together to make a cross.
3. Glue the fabric square to the middle of the cross to make the scarecrow's body.
4. Use a marker to draw a face on the circle.
5. Glue the circle on the cross, as shown, to make the head. Allow to dry.
6. Stick the scarecrow into the clay and fill your cup with raffia.

Scarecrow Puppet Pal

· ·

Materials For Each Child:
1 paper lunch bag
1 paint stirrer
newspaper
miscellaneous craft items (buttons, beads, fabric scraps, sponge, pompoms, rickrack, etc.)
glue

Class Preparations:
Obtain a class supply of paint stirrers from a local paint store or home supply warehouse. Have tape ready.

Directions:
1. Stuff the bag with newspaper.
2. Push the stirrer into the open end of the bag, gather the bag around the stirrer, and secure it with tape. Ⓣ
3. Glue craft items to the bag to make the scarecrow's facial features.

Leaf Creature

• •

Materials For Each Child:
1 sheet of 9" x 12" construction paper
4 leaves
2 craft beads or buttons, or wiggle eyes
crayons and glue

Class Preparations:
Have your youngsters collect a variety
of different-shaped leaves.

Directions:
1. Pick leaves from the collection to represent
a head, body, and ears.
2. Arrange the leaves on your paper to create
a leaf creature; then glue the leaves down.
3. Glue on beads for eyes, or use wiggle eyes.
4. Use crayons to add legs.

Trick-Or-Treat!

• •

Materials For Each Child:
½ apple
1 plain paper gift bag or kraft bag, with handles
orange tempera paint in a shallow dish
black marker

Class Preparations:
Cut several apples in half down the core to use for
printing. Pour orange paint into shallow dishes.

Directions:
1. Dip the flat side of the apple in the paint.
2. Press the painted side of the apple on the bag
(folded flat) to print a pumpkin shape. Cover one
side of the bag with pumpkin prints. Allow to dry.
3. Print pumpkins on the other side. Allow to dry.
4. Use a black marker to add faces to the
pumpkin shapes.

Get your youngsters into the Halloween spirit with these creepy classroom creations!

Jack-O'-Lantern

Materials For Each Child:
1 clay planting pot, 2" in diameter
orange tempera paint
black Slick® paint
length of yarn
paintbrushes

Class Preparations:
Purchase a classroom supply of 2" clay planting pots.

Directions:
1. To make a jack-o'-lantern, paint the rim of the clay pot orange; then, carefully turn the pot upside-down and paint the base orange.
2. When dry, use black Slick® paint to make a jack-o'-lantern's face on the side of the pot.
3. Tie a knot in one end of the yarn and thread it through the pot from the inside to hang it up. Ⓣ

Ghost Puppet

Materials For Each Child:
1 paper towel
1 cardboard tube
1 sheet of 12" x 18" white tissue paper
black marker

Class Preparations:
Have tape ready.

Directions:
1. Poke the paper towel into the tube.
2. Push part of the paper towel out the other end of the tube to form a ball which will become the ghost's head.
3. Drape tissue paper over the ghost's head and tape it in place around the top of the tube. Ⓗ
4. Add features with a black marker.

Mosaic Jack-O'-Lantern

Materials For Each Child:
1 sheet of 9" x 12" tagboard
tagboard jack-o'-lantern template, to share
dry orange lentils, green split peas, and
  black beans
pencil and glue

Class Preparations:
Enlarge the jack-o'-lantern pattern to make
tagboard templates for children to share.

Directions:
1. With a pencil, trace the jack-o'-lantern
template onto a sheet of tagboard.
2. Spread glue on the eyes, nose, and
mouth; then stick on black beans.
3. Apply glue to the rest of the jack-o'-lantern.
Cover it with orange lentils.
4. Spread glue over the background
and cover it with green split peas.
5. When the glue is dry,
gently shake the
picture to remove
loose pieces.

Glow In The Dark

· ·

Materials For Each Child:
1 sheet of 9" x 12" dark-colored construction
  paper, cut with slits
glitter, sequins, and/or Halloween stickers
1/2 sheet of 12" x 18" yellow tissue paper
1/2 sheet of 12" x 18" orange tissue paper
glue

Class Preparations:
Fold each child's sheet of construction paper in
half lengthwise, then cut a series of slits from the
folded edge to within 1 1/2" of the open edges,
as shown (A). Have a hole puncher and stapler
ready and yarn for hanging (optional).

Directions:
1. Unfold the paper; then spread glue along the
long edges and decorate with glitter, sequins,
and stickers.
2. Staple the shorter sides of the paper together
to make a cylinder (B). Ⓣ
3. Crumple the tissue paper loosely and push it
into the lantern to resemble a flame.
4. If desired, use a hole puncher to punch two
holes at the top of the lantern and insert a length
of yarn for hanging (C). Ⓣ
5. Put your lantern near a window or light so that
the light shines through it. Ⓣ

A
B
C

These dangly, spooky spiders are guaranteed to send a shiver down your spine! Ugh!

Creepy Cobweb

Materials For Each Child:
1 sheet of 9" x 12" dark-colored
  construction paper
8 narrow strips of black construction paper,
  2" in length
1 egg-carton cup
4 white paper straws, cut in half
2 wiggle eyes
black and white tempera paints
paintbrushes and glue

Class Preparations:
Cut egg cartons to provide each child with one egg cup. Then cut black construction paper into strips so that each child has eight for his spider's legs. Cut straws in half.

Directions:
1. Glue straws to a sheet of paper to make the spokes of the cobweb, as shown. ⒣
2. Complete the cobweb by painting white lines between the straws. ⒣
3. To make the spider's body, paint the outside of the egg-carton cup black. Allow to dry.
4. Glue eight paper legs on the egg-carton. Allow the glue to dry.
5. Glue wiggle eyes on top of the spider.
6. Attach the spider to the web by gluing the ends of several legs to the paper. ⒣

Spider Splat

Materials For Each Child:
1 sheet of 9" x 12" white or light-colored
  construction paper
1 straw
2 wiggle eyes
thinned black tempera paint and paintbrush
glue

Directions:
1. Use a paintbrush to drip a blob of black paint onto your paper.
2. Make eight long legs by blowing through a straw, sending the paint in different directions. Allow to dry.
3. Glue wiggle eyes to the spider's body.

24

I Spy A Spider

Materials For Each Child:
1 square of 12" x 12" black crepe paper
1 sheet of newspaper
1 piece of yarn, about 14" in length
4 black pipe cleaners, 8" in length, cut in half
1 piece of thread, to hang up spider
2 big wiggle eyes and glue

Class Preparations:
For each child, cut crepe paper into a 12"
square and cut four pipe cleaners in half.
Have masking tape ready.

Directions:
1. Crumple a sheet of newspaper tightly
into a ball.
2. Wrap masking tape around the ball to
keep it in shape. ⓣ
3. Place the ball on crepe paper and gather
up the edges. Tie yarn around the edges. ⓣ
4. Tuck the pipe cleaners under the yarn to
make the legs. ⓗ
5. Glue on big wiggle eyes.
6. Tape a piece of thread to the top of the
spider for hanging. ⓗ

Spunky Spider

Materials For Each Child:
2 Styrofoam® egg-carton cups
4 black pipe cleaners, 8" in length
2 wiggle eyes
1 rubberband, cut and knotted at one end
black tempera paint and paintbrush
glue

Class Preparations:
Cut Styrofoam® egg cartons so that each child
has two adjoining egg cups. Use scissors to
poke four holes along each side. Cut apart a
class supply of rubberbands; tie a knot in one
end of each. Have a pencil ready.

Directions:
1. Paint the spider's egg-cup body black.
2. Poke each pipe cleaner through both sides
of the body and bend to make legs. ⓗ
3. Glue on wiggle eyes.
4. Make a small hole with a pencil between the
two egg cups. Thread the rubberband through
the hole. ⓣ

Batty Door Handle

Materials For Each Child:
2 black tagboard bat cutouts
1 pipe cleaner, 12" in length
colored crayons
glitter and glue

Class Preparations:
Trace around the bat pattern on the right and cut out two tagboard bats for each child. Have tape ready.

Directions:
1. Decorate the bats with colored crayons.
2. Add glue and sprinkle on glitter. Allow to dry.
3. Bend the pipe cleaner in half.
4. Tape the bats to each end of the pipe cleaner, as shown. Ⓗ
5. Hang the bats over your bedroom door knob.

Lucky Black Cat

Materials For Each Child:
1 black construction-paper cat head cutout
1 paper cup (9 oz.)
green glitter
black pipe cleaner
black tempera paint and paintbrush
pencil and glue

Class Preparations:
Use the pattern below to cut out a black construction-paper head for each child. Use a cup for the cat's body. Cut four notches in each cup to make four legs.

Directions:
1. Paint the cup black and allow to dry.
2. Put two circles of glue on the cat's head and sprinkle on glitter to make the eyes. Allow to dry.
3. Glue the head to the cup.
4. Make a hole in the top of the cup, with a pencil and poke the pipe cleaner up through it. Bend it to look like a tail.

Celebrate Thanksgiving by making festive turkey decorations.

Turkey On A Plate

Materials For Each Child:
1 orange construction-paper beak
1 red construction-paper wattle
1 paper plate, 10" in diameter
1 small, white plastic cup
2 wiggle eyes
brown tempera paint and paintbrush
black fine-tip marker and glue

Class Preparations:
For each child, cut the rim off a paper plate to make a flat circle. Cut an orange paper diamond for a beak and a red paper wattle.

Directions:
1. Glue the cup upside-down near the edge of the plate to make a head, as shown.
2. Paint feathers around the plate. When dry, draw a black line through the center of each feather.
3. Fold the orange paper diamond in half to make a triangular beak. Glue one side to the cup so that it opens like a beak.
4. Glue on wiggle eyes and a red paper wattle for a finishing touch.

Tootsy Turkeys

Materials For Each Child:
1 sheet of 12" x 18" construction paper
brown tempera paint mixed with liquid soap in a shallow tray
tempera paints or pencils in fall colors
paintbrushes
black marker

Class Preparations:
Mix brown paint with a little liquid soap in a shallow tray. Provide a tub of water to wash up and towels to dry feet.

Directions:
1. Have each child put one bare foot in the tray of paint, then on a sheet of construction paper. ⓗ
2. Allow the print to dry.
3. With the toes facing down, draw or paint feathers around the foot in other fall colors.
4. Use a marker and paint to add facial features to the footprint to resemble a turkey.

Learn about Native-American crafts and traditions, such as wampum—colored beads made from shells.

Indian Corn

Materials For Each Child:
1 white construction-paper corncob cutout
2 green construction-paper husk cutouts
red, orange, yellow, brown, and black
   tempera paints in shallow dishes
glue

Class Preparations:
Use the pattern on page 30 to cut out a corncob from white construction paper and two husks from green construction paper for each child. Pour paint into shallow dishes.

Directions:
1. Dip your finger into a color of paint and press onto the corncob cutout.
2. Continue in this manner, using different colors until the cutout is covered.
3. When the paint is dry, glue on the green construction-paper husks, as shown. 🅗

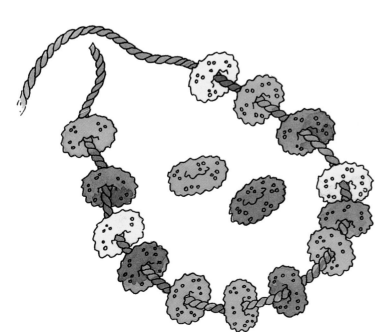

Wampum Necklace

Materials For Each Child:
1 piece of yarn, 18" in length
Fruit Loops® cereal

Class Preparations:
For each child, tape one end of a piece of yarn to keep it from unraveling.

Directions:
1. String Fruit Loops® onto a strand of yarn to make a pattern.
2. Remove the tape and tie the ends of the yarn together to make a necklace. 🅗

29

fall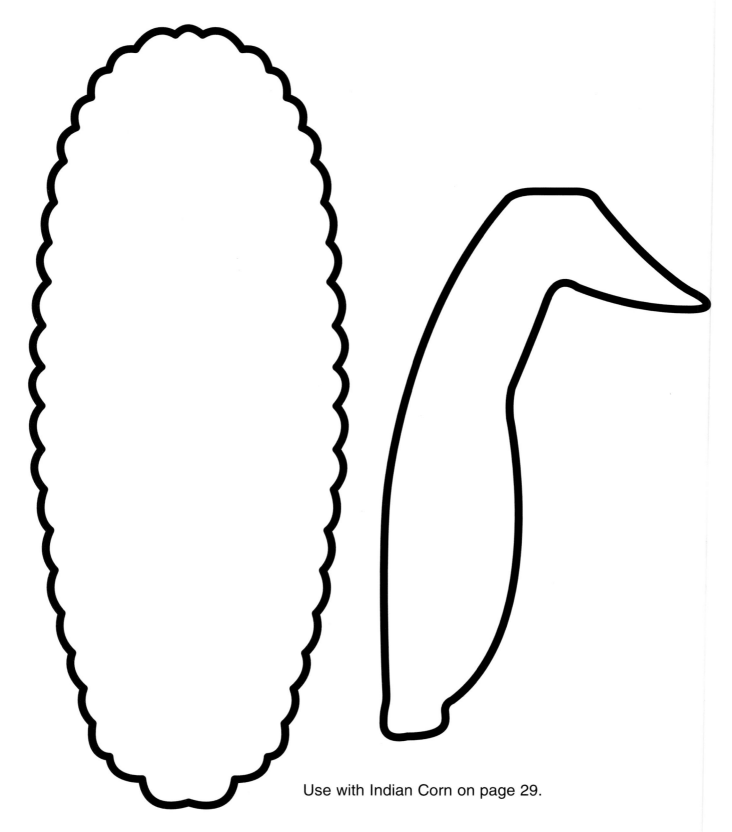

Use with Indian Corn on page 29.

Story Belt

Materials For Each Child:
1 strip of 4" x 18" tagboard
1 strip of 3" x 14" white construction paper
2 pieces of yarn, to tie belt around child's waist
colored pasta shells
pencil and glue

Class Preparations:
To make imitation wampum beads, mix half
a cup of rubbing alcohol, a few drops of food
coloring, and one cup of small pasta shells in
a separate container for each color desired.
When they are thoroughly covered with the
colored mixture, remove them from the liquid;
then spread them out on paper towels to
dry overnight. Cut the tagboard and paper
into strips. Have a hole puncher ready.

Explain to your students that Native Americans
sewed wampum beads onto belts to record
stories. Have each child think of a story and
decorate the belt with her idea.

Directions:
1. Glue the colored shells onto the tagboard
to form characters or designs.
2. When the glue dries, write or dictate a
sentence about your wampum belt on the
construction-paper strip. Ⓣ
3. Glue the paper strip to the back of the belt.
4. Use a hole puncher to make a hole in each
end of the belt. Thread a length of yarn through
each hole in the belt and tie it securely. Ⓣ
5. Tie the belt around your waist and tell
the class about your belt. Ⓗ

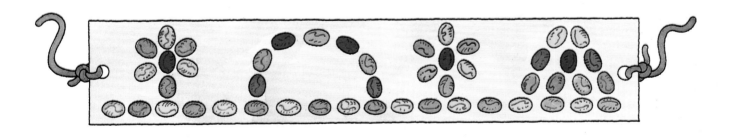

The sun helps things grow.

fall

Native American Rattle

Materials For Each Child:
1 strip of construction paper, to fit around can
1 small frozen juice can with lid
several different sponge shapes, to share
bean and corn seeds
different-colored tempera paints in
   shallow dishes
spoon and glue

Class Preparations:
Collect an empty frozen juice can and its lid for each child. Cut a strip of construction paper to fit around each can. Put a variety of bean and corn seeds into a container. Prepare dishes of paint and several different sponge shapes.

Directions:
1. Use the sponge to paint designs on the strip of construction paper. Allow to dry.
2. Glue the paper around a can. **(H)**
3. Place a few spoonfuls of seed mixture into the can; then glue the lid in place.
4. When the glue dries, shake the can to make simple rhythmic sounds.

Native American Bags

Materials For Each Child:
1 lunch bag
1 piece of yarn, about 20" in length
colored markers or tempera paints
paintbrushes and glue

Class Preparations:
For each child, cut off the top of a lunch bag and cut a fringe along the scrap. Explain that, long ago, many Native American men carried decorated bags made from deer or buffalo skin. After showing a variety of photographs, give each child an opportunity to make a decorated bag. Have a hole puncher ready.

Directions:
1. Glue a fringe to the bottom of a bag.
2. Use markers or paints to decorate the bag.
3. Use a hole puncher to punch two holes in the top of the bag; then tie on a length of yarn to make a strap. **(T)**

As fall draws to an end, explain to your students how different animals prepare for the winter ahead.

Swish Your Bushy Tail!

Materials For Each Child:
1 sheet of 12" x 18" white construction paper
1 gray construction-paper squirrel cutout
leaf
hazelnut
gray tempera paint in a shallow dish
glue

Class Preparations:
For each child, duplicate the squirrel pattern on page 34 onto gray construction paper and cut out. Pour gray paint into a shallow dish.

Directions:
1. Glue the squirrel cutout onto a sheet of white construction paper.
2. Dip one side of a leaf into the gray paint and use it to print a bushy tail, as shown.
3. Glue a hazelnut between the squirrel's paws.

fall

Use with Swish Your Bushy Tail!
on page 33.

34

Prickly Porcupine

Materials For Each Child:
brown and black cornstarch clay
several short lengths of dry spaghetti

Class Preparations:
Make a batch of cornstarch clay (see recipe on page 5). Add tempera paint to color most of the clay brown. Reserve a small portion and color it black.

Directions:
1. Mold a piece of brown clay into a ball to make the porcupine's body.
2. Add small balls of black clay for the nose and eyes.
3. Push short lengths of spaghetti into the porcupine's back to make quills.

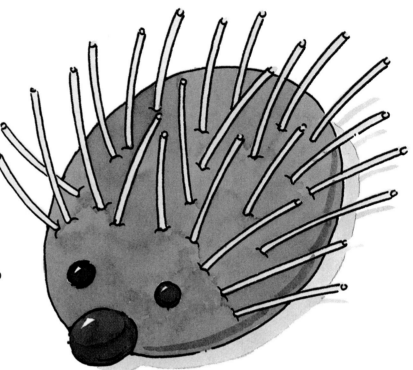

"Wowl!"

Materials For Each Child:
1 sheet of construction paper, with owl outline
brown, black, and gray tissue-paper pieces, cut into 1½" squares
crayons and glue

Class Preparations:
Duplicate the owl pattern on page 36 on construction paper for each child. Cut a supply of brown, black, and gray tissue-paper squares, 1½" x 1½"

Directions:
1. Color the owl's face with crayons and draw on features.
2. Glue the top of each tissue-paper piece onto the owl's body in layers to resemble feathers.
3. Draw feet, as shown, with a black crayon.

Use with "Wowl!" on page 35.

winter

Winter Bird Feeder

Materials For Each Child:
1 clean, dry milk carton
birdseed
pencil and length of string

Class Preparations:
Save milk cartons from school lunches. Rinse and allow to dry. Have scissors and a hole puncher ready.

Directions:
1. Cut the top off the carton.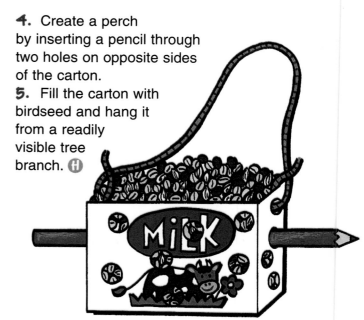
2. Use a pencil to make randomly placed holes along the side panels of the carton.
3. Also punch two holes on opposite sides of the carton and tie string through the holes.

4. Create a perch by inserting a pencil through two holes on opposite sides of the carton.
5. Fill the carton with birdseed and hang it from a readily visible tree branch.

Hanukkah Candles

Materials For Each Child:
1 square of yellow tissue paper, 6" x 6"
1 square of orange tissue paper, 6" x 6"
1 cardboard tube
tempera paints in bright colors
paintbrushes

Class Preparations:
For this group project, cut a square, 6" x 6", from both yellow and orange tissue paper for each child.

Directions:
1. Paint different designs on a cardboard tube using bright colors. Allow the paint to dry.
2. Crumple up together one orange and one yellow tissue-paper square and push them into one end of the tube to make a candle flame.
3. Arrange the class candles in a row as a menorah with the center candle on a block to make it taller.

Your students will love the hidden candies in this delicious variation on an Advent calendar.

Treeful Of Surprises

Materials For Each Child:
1 colored construction-paper semicircle
1 tagboard handle, labeled with
 child's name
1 piece of wrapped candy
glitter and glue

Class Preparations:
For this group project, use the pattern on page 40 to cut out a colored semicircle for each child. Number the semicircles 1 through 24. Cut a strip of tagboard about 3/4" x 6" to make a handle for each cone. Label each cone handle with the name of a child in your class. Stand a large twiggy branch in a flowerpot filled with soil. Have a stapler and tape ready.

Directions:
1. Spread glue along the curved edge of the semicircle and sprinkle on glitter. Allow the glue to dry.
2. Tape the semicircle into a cone; then staple on the tagboard handle. **T**
3. Put a piece of wrapped candy in each cone.
4. Hang the cones on the twig tree. **H**
5. Each day of December, remove the cone with that day's date on it, and give it to the child named on the handle. **T**

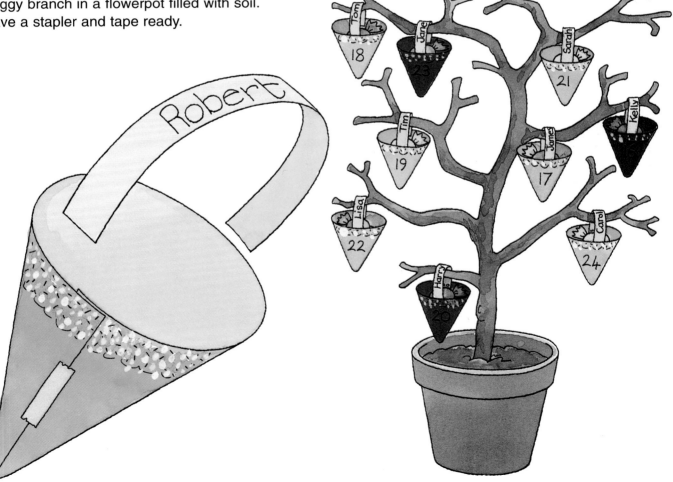

Greetings!

Materials For Each Child:
¹/₆ sheet of 12" x 18" white
  construction paper
Christmas giftwrap scraps
glue

Class Preparations:
For this group project, decide on a festive greeting and write each of the letters in the greeting on a separate 6" square of paper. Provide each child with one letter. Have clothespins and a length of string or clothesline ready to hang the letters.

Directions:
1. Tear giftwrap into small pieces.
2. Spread glue on the letter and stick on the scraps of giftwrap.
3. Use clothespins to hang the letters on a long line. ⓣ

Use with Treeful Of Surprises on page 39, Chirpees on page 98, and Squeak, Squeak on page 138.

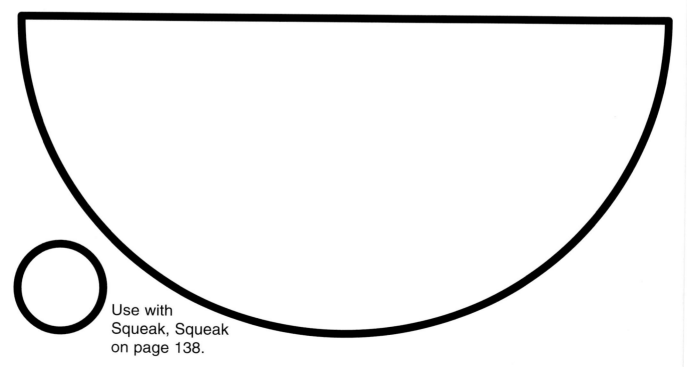

Use with
Squeak, Squeak
on page 138.

These Christmas cards have a special twist. They are sure to impress your students' family and friends!

Snowman Card

Materials For Each Child:
$1/3$ sheet of 12" x 18" dark construction paper
3 small buttons
half a large, round potato
tinsel
white tempera paint in a shallow container
black fine-tip marker
pencil and glue

Class Preparations:
For each child, cut a 12" x 6" piece of construction paper. Fold it in half to make a square card, 6" x 6". Cut the potatoes in half.

Directions:
1. Dip the flat side of half a potato in the paint and use it to print the snowman's head and body on the card.
2. Print snowflakes with the blunt end of a pencil. Allow the paint to dry.
3. Glue on the buttons; then glue on tinsel for a scarf.
4. Use a marker to draw a snowman face.

Sparkle Paint Christmas Card

Materials For Each Child:
$1/3$ sheet of 12" x 18" colored construction paper
1 cup each of flour, water, salt, and powdered tempera paint for each color
empty dish-detergent bottle or paint bottle with a nozzle for each color

Class Preparations:
For each child, cut a 12" x 6" piece of construction paper. Fold it in half to make a square card, 6" x 6". You may wish to organize the children into groups to make different colors of sparkle paint.

Directions:
1. Mix together the flour, water, salt, and paint. Pour the mixture into a bottle. Mix several colors. ⓗ
2. Squeeze the thick paints out of each bottle slowly to make a design on your card.
3. Allow your card to dry overnight.

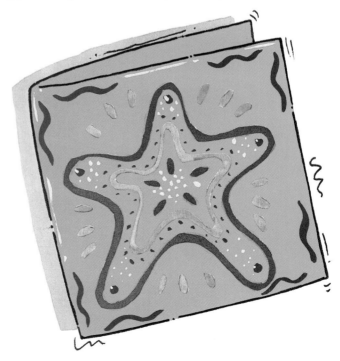

Have the students help you put up a classroom Christmas tree. Here are some great ideas for decorations!

Beads For The Tree

Materials For Each Child:
several 4" squares of double-sided,
  colored construction paper
thick-handled paintbrush
long length of cord
glue

Class Preparations:
Glue sheets of different-colored 12" x 18" construction paper together back to back. Allow the paper to dry overnight. Then tear the paper into squares, approximately 4" x 4". Give each child a handful of squares.

Directions:
1. Roll a paper square into a tube shape around a paintbrush.
2. Glue the end of the paper down, to make a cylindrical bead. (H)
3. Keep making beads until you have used up all the squares of paper.
4. Thread all the beads onto cord and tie the ends together. Use the beads to decorate your Christmas tree. (T)

Pretzel Garland

Materials For Each Child:
1 yard of narrow ribbon
12 small pretzels

Class Preparations:
Tie a pretzel to one end of the ribbon to stop the other pretzels from falling off when they are being threaded.

Directions:
1. Carefully thread the ribbon in and out of the pretzels as shown to make a garland. (H)
2. Tie the end of the ribbon to the last pretzel. (T)
3. Use your pretzel garland to decorate your classroom bulletin board or hang it on a Christmas tree. If you use unsalted pretzels, you can decorate trees outdoors so that the birds can enjoy a tasty snack. (H)

Hear The Bells!

Materials For Each Child:
2 craft foam bell cutouts
2 narrow ribbons, each 6" in length
1 jingle bell
glue

Class Preparations:
Use the pattern below to cut two bell shapes from craft foam for each child. Use a hole puncher to make a hole at the top of each bell shape.

Directions:
1. Thread the jingle bell onto a length of ribbon.
2. Put a line of glue down the middle of one of the foam bells and lay the ribbon along it, so that the jingle bell pokes out at the bottom (A).
3. Glue the second foam bell on top of the first, so that the ribbon is sandwiched between the two bell shapes.
4. Thread another ribbon through the holes at the top of the bell (B).
5. Tie a knot in the ribbon and hang the bell on a Christmas tree.

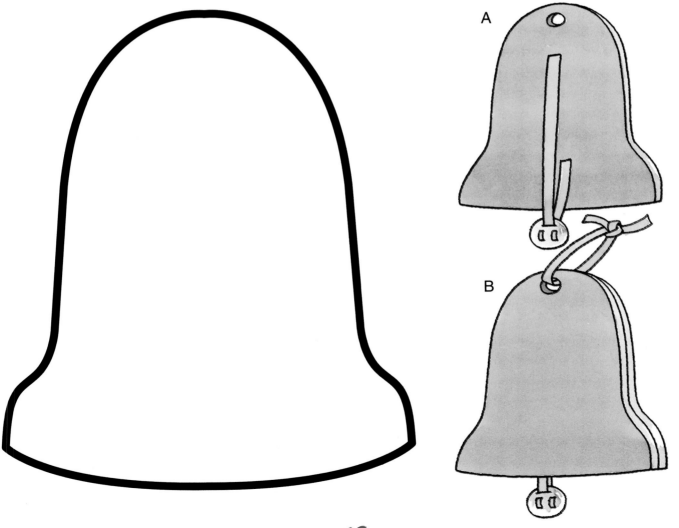

Candy Twist
Tree Decoration

Materials For Each Child:
1 red pipe cleaner
1 white pipe cleaner
wide ribbon

Directions:
1. Twist together a red and a white pipe cleaner.
2. Bend over the end of the pipe-cleaner twist to make a handle.
3. Tie a piece of ribbon in a bow around the decoration. (T)
4. Attach to a Christmas gift or hang on a Christmas tree. (H)

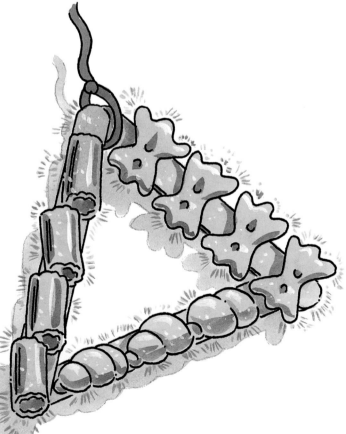

Pasta Pretty

Materials For Each Child:
3 craft sticks, glued together
dry pasta shapes, such as shells, bows, and tubes
length of gold thread
gold and silver tempera paints
paintbrush
glitter
glue

Class Preparations:
For each child, use a hot glue gun to glue three craft sticks together to form a triangle.

Directions:
1. Glue pasta shapes onto your triangle.
2. Paint the triangle with gold or silver paint.
3. Sprinkle on glitter while the paint is wet.
4. Allow the triangle to dry.
5. Tie gold thread, as shown, to hang. (T)

44

Star Shine

• • • • • • • • • • • • • • •

Materials For Each Child:
1 tagboard star cutout
1 piece of aluminum foil, 10" square
narrow ribbon, 6" in length
paintbrush
glitter and glue

Class Preparations:
Use the pattern below to cut a tagboard star
for each child. Have a hole puncher ready.

Directions:
1. Wrap foil around the star to cover
all the tagboard. ⊞
2. Use a paintbrush to make a pattern
with glue on the star; then sprinkle on glitter.
3. Use a hole puncher to punch a hole
through one point. ⓣ
4. Thread narrow ribbon through
the hole; then tie a bow. ⓣ
5. Hang the star on
a Christmas tree. ⊞

Use with Star Shine
on this page, Christmas
Frames on page 54,
Patriotic Mobile on page
118, and Magic Wand
on page 136.

45

Danglers

· · · · · · · · · · · · ·

Materials For Each Child:
1 paper cup
narrow ribbon
glitter in a saucer
beads
tempera paint and paintbrush
glue in a saucer

Class Preparations:
For this group project, collect a class supply of paper cups. Make a small hole in the bottom of each cup. Pour glitter and glue into separate saucers. Have string ready for hanging.

Directions:
1. Paint the paper cup and allow to dry.
2. Dip the rim of the cup into glue and then into the glitter. Allow to dry.
3. To make a class decoration, thread all the danglers onto string, with beads in between them. (H)
4. Tie ribbons to the string. (T)
5. Hang the string of decorations from the ceiling or door. (T)

Christmas Wreath

· ·

Materials For Each Child:
1 paper plate, 10" in diameter
dry pasta shapes, some painted gold and silver
length of ribbon
green, red, and white tempera paints
paintbrushes and glue

Class Preparations:
For each child, cut out the center of a paper plate and use a hole puncher to punch a hole near the edge. Use spray paints to paint a handful of small dried pasta shapes gold and silver.

Directions:
1. Paint the paper plate green.
2. Paint some dry pasta shapes red and white. Allow the paint to dry.
3. Thread ribbon through the hole in the plate. (H)
4. Decorate your plate by gluing on the red, white, gold, and silver pasta shapes.

Deck The Tree

. . . .

Materials For Each Child:
½ sheet of 9" x 12" green construction paper
beads, popcorn, and glitter
tempera paints in various colors
paintbrushes
glue

Class Preparations:
For each child, cut a piece of 9" x 6"
construction paper and fold in half lengthwise,
Use the pattern below, putting the dotted edge
on the paper fold, and cut out the tree shape.

Directions:
1. Paint some popcorn with tempera paints and
allow it to dry.
2. Open out your tree and decorate it by gluing
on beads, popcorn, and glitter. Be careful not to
glue anything along the center fold.
3. Fold your tree to stand it up.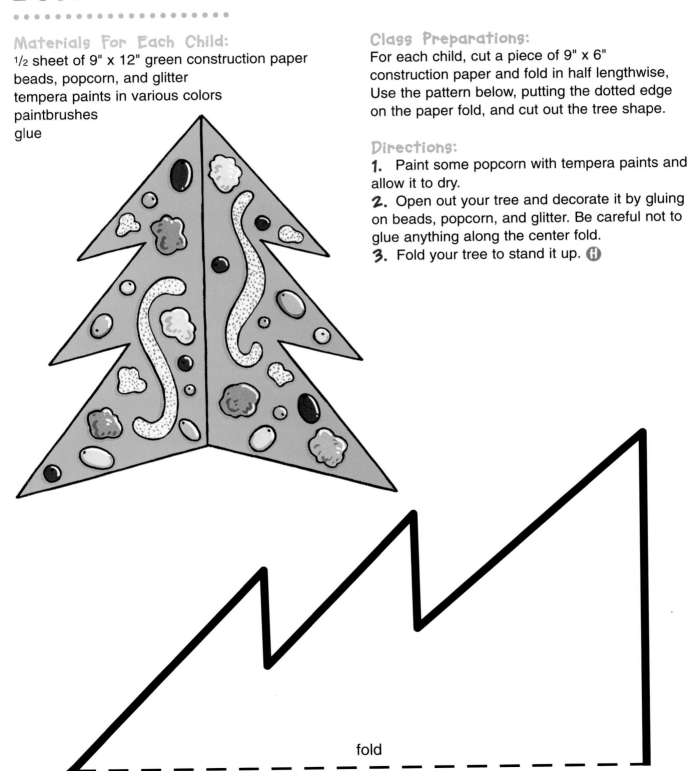

fold

Mini Tree

- - - - - - - - - - - - -

Materials For Each Child:
1 green construction-paper semicircle
1 cardboard tube
candy, beads, tinsel, and glitter
brown tempera paint
paintbrush
glue

Class Preparations:
Use the larger pattern on the opposite page
to cut a semicircle from green construction
paper for each child. Have tape ready.

Directions:
1. Bend the semicircle into a cone shape
and tape the edges.
2. Decorate the cone by gluing on candy,
beads, tinsel, and glitter. Allow to dry.
3. Paint the cardboard tube brown. Allow
the paint to dry.
4. Balance the cone
on its tube trunk.

Santa Claus

- - - - - - - - - - - - - - - - - -

Materials For Each Child:
1 large flesh-colored construction-paper
   cone
1 small red construction-paper cone
cotton
black and red markers and glue

Class Preparations:
Use the semicircle patterns on the opposite
page to trace a large flesh-colored
semicircle for Santa's face and a smaller,
red semicircle for Santa's hat for each
child. Tape the semicircles to make cones.
Have thread and tape ready for hanging.

Directions:
1. Glue the small cone on top of the large
cone to make Santa's face and hat.
2. Use markers to draw black eyes and
a red nose on Santa's face.
3. Glue on cotton eyebrows and a beard.
4. Push a loop of thread through the
top of the cones and tape inside to
hang the Santa.

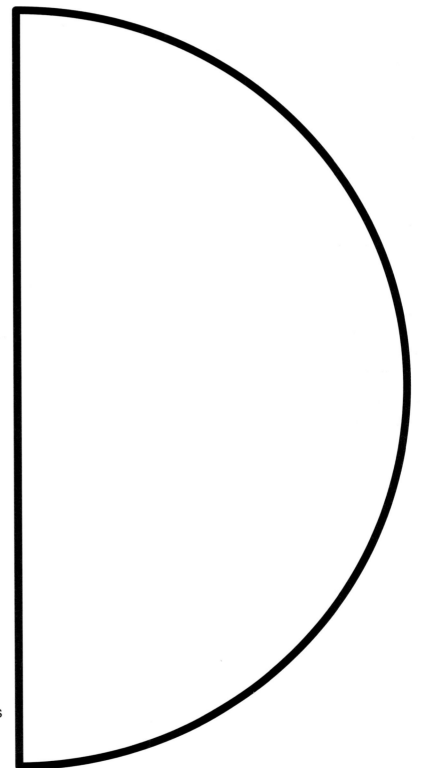

Use with Santa
Claus on page 48.

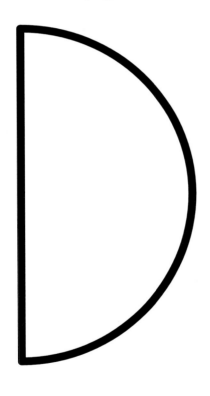

Use with Santa Claus
and Mini Tree on
page 48.

Paper-Chain Plate

Materials For Each Child:
1 paper plate, 10" in diameter
12 gummed-paper strips
3 jingle bells
tempera paints
paintbrushes

Class Preparations:
For each child, use a hole puncher to punch two holes in opposite sides of a paper plate, as shown. Have string and tape ready.

Directions:
1. Paint the plate and allow to dry.
2. Thread a length of string through the holes in the plate, as shown, and knot the ends. ⓣ
3. Make three short lengths of paper chain using the gummed-paper strips.
4. Thread string through the hole in a jingle bell and tie the bell onto the bottom of each chain. ⓣ
5. Tape all three chains to the underside of the plate. ⓗ
6. Hang the decoration from the ceiling. ⓣ

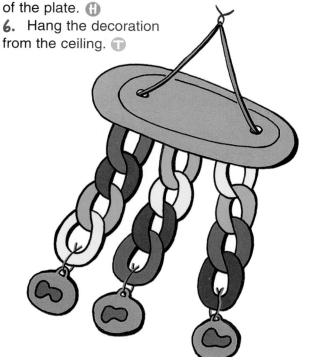

Santa Centerpiece

Materials For Each Child:
1 clean milk carton, with the top cut off
1 piece of white construction paper, large enough to fit around a milk carton
twigs, holly leaves, and evergreen pieces
cotton balls
colored markers and glue

Class Preparations:
For each child, cut the top off a milk carton. Cut a piece of white paper to fit around each carton.

Directions:
1. Glue the white paper around the milk carton. ⓗ
2. Use markers to draw eyes, a nose, and mouth on the carton.
3. Glue on cotton balls for Santa's beard and around the top of the carton for Santa's hair.
4. Arrange some twigs, holly leaves, and evergreen pieces in your centerpiece.

My Own Snowman

Materials For Each Child:
1 large and 1 small Styrofoam® ball
markers
2–3 buttons or beads
paper plate
cotton balls
glitter
glue

Directions:
1. Use markers to draw eyes, a nose, and a mouth on the small Styrofoam® ball.
2. Glue the two Styrofoam® balls together to make a snowman, as shown.
3. Decorate the snowman by gluing on buttons or beads.
4. Glue the bottom of the snowman to an upturned paper plate.
5. Glue cotton balls around the base of the snowman and sprinkle with a little glitter to look like frosty snow.

Plate Snowman

Materials For Each Child:
1 paper-plate snowman
1 orange gummed-paper triangle
black gummed-paper dots
gold cord and 2 lengths of ribbon

Class Preparations:
For each child, staple two 7" plates together to form a snowman shape. Use a hole puncher to punch holes around the edge of the snowman's body and one at the top of the head. Cut a triangle of orange gummed paper for each snowman's nose.

Directions:
1. Stick on black gummed dots for the snowman's eyes, mouth, and buttons, and an orange triangle for a nose.
2. Thread gold cord through the holes around the snowman's body. (H)
3. Tie a ribbon as a scarf around the snowman's neck. (T)
4. Thread a ribbon through the hole at the top of the head. Tie a knot to hang. (T)

Silly Snowman Finger Puppet

∙ ∙

Materials For Each Child:
1 white tagboard snowman cutout
colored markers
a length of ribbon

Class Preparations:
Use the pattern on the opposite page to cut a snowman shape from tagboard for each child. Cut holes for fingers at the bottom.

Directions:
1. Use markers to draw eyes, a nose, a mouth, and a hat on your snowman.
2. Tie a ribbon around the snowman's neck for a scarf. ⓣ
3. Push two of your fingers through the holes and wiggle them to make the snowman move around.

Snowman Mask

∙ ∙

Materials For Each Child:
1 colored tagboard hat cutout
1 orange construction-paper triangle
2 black construction-paper circles
1 paper plate, 7" in diameter
1 craft stick or tongue depressor
white cotton balls and glue

Class Preparations:
Use the patterns on the opposite page to cut a hat from tagboard for each child. Also, cut one orange triangle and two black circles from construction paper. Have tape ready.

Directions:
1. Glue cotton balls on a paper plate to cover it. Glue the hat cutout to the top of the plate.
2. Glue on an orange triangle for a nose, and two black circles for eyes, as shown.
3. Tape a craft stick or tongue depressor to the back of the mask as a handle. ⓗ

Use with Snowman Mask
on page 52.

Use with Snowman Mask
on page 52.

Use with Snowman Mask on
page 52 and Reindeer Bag
on page 58.

Use with Silly Snowman Finger Puppet
on page 52.

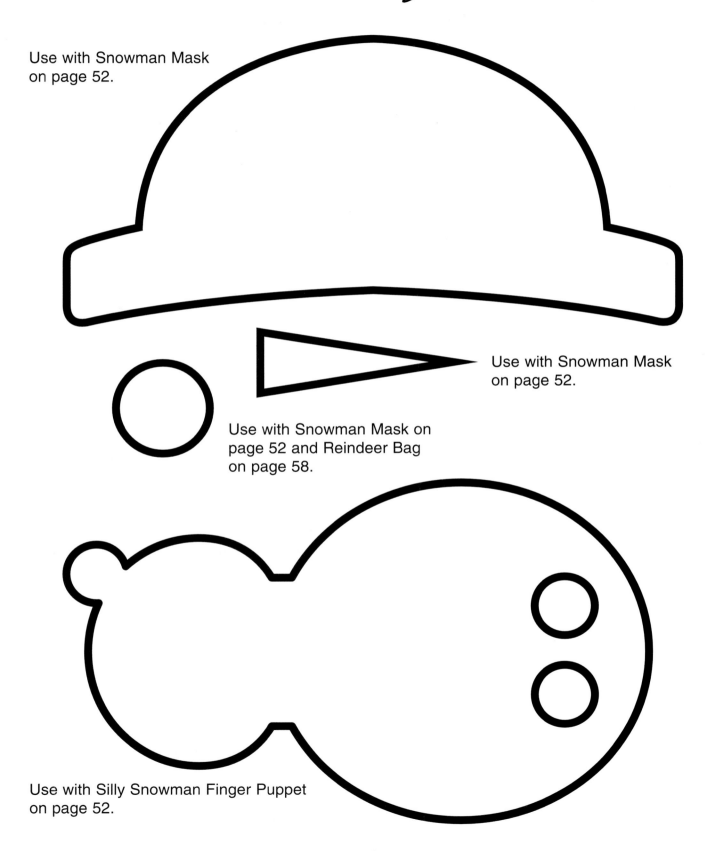

Frosty Shapes

. . . .

Materials For Each Child:
5 posterboard cutouts
1 sheet of 12" x 18" blue construction paper
Sticky Tac®
sponge
white tempera paint in a shallow dish

Class Preparations:
Use the tree, snowman, and holly leaf patterns on the opposite page to cut five patterns from posterboard for each child. Pour paint into shallow dishes.

Directions:
1. Use small pieces of Sticky Tac® to stick the Christmas shapes on a sheet of blue construction paper. ⓗ
2. Use a sponge to dab white paint all over the blue paper, and over the shapes. Allow the paint to dry.
3. Lift the shapes off the paper to reveal the unpainted areas. ⓗ

Christmas Frames

. . . .

Materials For Each Child:
2 gold or silver posterboard star cutouts
an individual school photo
sequins
tempera paints and paintbrushes
glue

Class Preparations:
Use the pattern on page 45 to cut out two stars from gold or silver posterboard for each child. Cut out a circular window in one star and trim each child's photo to fit. Have a loop of ribbon ready for each child. Cover work surfaces with newspaper.

Directions:
1. Use a paintbrush to spatter paint onto one side of the star with the window. Allow to dry.
2. Glue on sequins.
3. Position a photo behind the window.
4. Glue the second star behind the photo.
5. Fold the ribbon into a loop and glue to the back of the star. ⓣ
6. Hang on a Christmas tree or use as a gift tag. ⓗ

Use with Frosty Shapes on page 54.

A smiling angel will add the finishing touch to your festive tree. It will make a pretty table centerpiece, too.

Angel Wings

Materials For Each Child:

1 tagboard circle
1 doily, cut into three sections
short lengths of yellow yarn
black fine-tip marker
glue

Class Preparations:

For each child, cut a tagboard circle for an angel's face, using a jar lid, 2" in diameter, as a template. Fold a doily in half and half again. Open out. Then, using the fold lines as a guide, cut out one quarter of the doily, as shown (A). Fold the quarter in half. Again, use the fold line as a guide to cut the quarter to make two wings (B). Have tape ready.

Directions:

1. Twist the large piece of doily into a cone and tape together. (H)
2. Glue or tape the two small doily pieces to the back of the cone as wings. (H)
3. Use a marker to draw a face on the circle and glue on yarn for hair. Glue the face to the top of the cone.

What An Angel!

Materials For Each Child:
2 construction-paper wing cutouts
1 construction-paper circle cutout
1 empty detergent bottle, wrapped
   in white construction paper
glitter
colored markers
paintbrush and glue

Class Preparations:
For each child, wrap an empty detergent
bottle in white construction paper, as shown.
Also, use the patterns below to cut a pair of
wings and a circle from construction paper.

Directions:
1. Use markers to draw a face and hair
on the circle.
2. Glue a face and wings on the bottle,
as shown.
3. To decorate the angel, paint on glue
in stars and curls; then sprinkle with glitter.

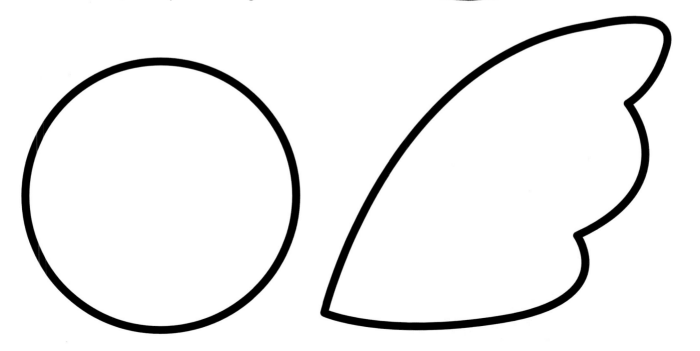

Reindeer Bag

Materials For Each Child:

½ sheet of 9" x 12" white tagboard
1 brown construction-paper reindeer head cutout
1 red construction-paper circle, 2" in diameter
2 white construction-paper circles, 1" in diameter
brown paper lunch bag
black sticky dots
pencil and glue

Class Preparations:

Use the pattern below to cut a reindeer head from brown construction paper for each child. Use a jar lid as a template to cut a circle, 2" in diameter, from red construction paper for a nose. Use the template on page 53 to cut two white circles, 1" in diameter, for eyes. Have scissors ready.

Directions:

1. Use a pencil to draw around each of your hands onto white tagboard.
2. Cut out the handprints to make antlers. Ⓣ
3. Glue the antlers behind the brown construction-paper head. Glue on the white circles for eyes, then stick on black dots to make pupils.
4. Glue the brown construction-paper head onto the back of the bag, so that it sticks up above the bag, as shown.
5. Glue the red circle for a nose on the front of the bag, as shown.
6. Fill your reindeer bag with Christmas treats, candy corn, or popped corn.

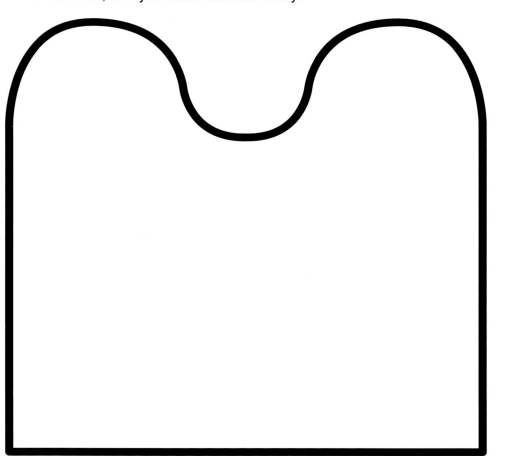

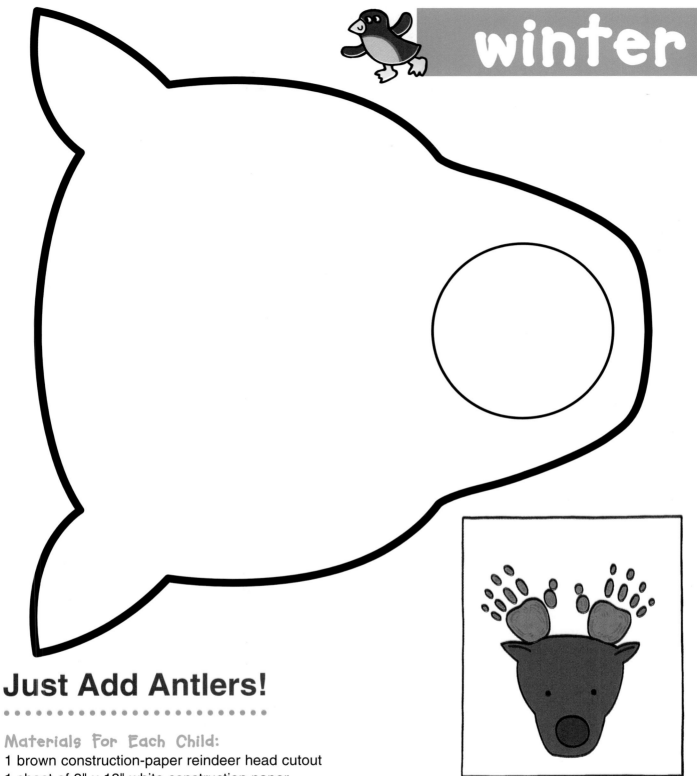

Just Add Antlers!

Materials For Each Child:
1 brown construction-paper reindeer head cutout
1 sheet of 9" x 12" white construction paper
brown tempera paint in shallow tray
colored markers
glue

Class Preparations:
Use the pattern above to cut out a reindeer head for each child from brown construction paper.

Directions:
1. Glue the reindeer head onto the white construction paper.
2. Dip both hands in the paint and press them down above the reindeer head to print antlers. Allow the paint to dry.
3. Use markers to add features to the reindeer.

When it snows, why not talk to your students about animals that live in frozen conditions all year long?

Hide-and-Seek Bears

• •

Materials For Each Child:
1 white construction-paper polar bear cutout
1 sheet of 9" x 12" white construction paper
white tissue-paper scraps
black fine-tip marker
glue

Class Preparations:
Use the pattern above to cut out a polar bear from construction paper for each child.

Directions:
1. Use a black fine-tip marker to draw features on the polar bear.
2. Put a small circle of glue on the back of the polar bear and stick it onto the sheet of white construction paper.
3. Crumple scraps of tissue paper into balls and glue them to the background to make falling snow around the bear.

Penguin Card

Materials For Each Child:
1 white construction-paper penguin front cutout
1 white construction-paper penguin pouch cutout
1 black construction-paper penguin body cutout
1 orange construction-paper beak
2 wiggle eyes
message written on a paper scrap
glue

Class Preparations:
Use the pattern below to cut a penguin's front from white construction paper for each child. Use the pattern on page 62 to cut the penguin's pouch from white paper. Fold a strip of 6" x 18" black paper in half widthwise. Use the pattern on page 62 to draw a penguin shape, butting the head up to the fold. Cut out the penguin, but do not cut along the fold. Also, cut a beak from an orange construction-paper scrap. Write messages on paper scraps to place in each penguin's pouch.

Directions:
1. Glue the white front to the black penguin.
2. Glue on wiggle eyes and a beak.
3. Spread glue around the edges of the pouch and stick it onto the penguin's tummy, leaving the top open to slip in a message.
4. Stand up your penguin card.
5. Slip a message into the pouch.

Penguin front

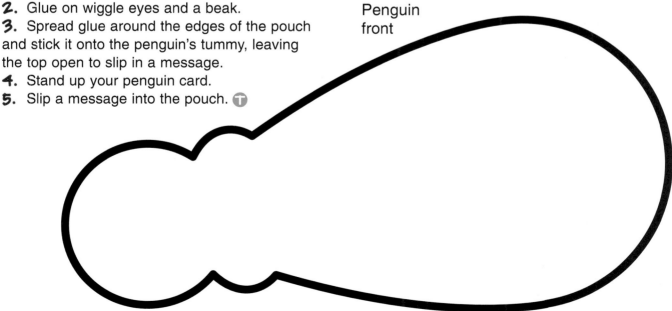

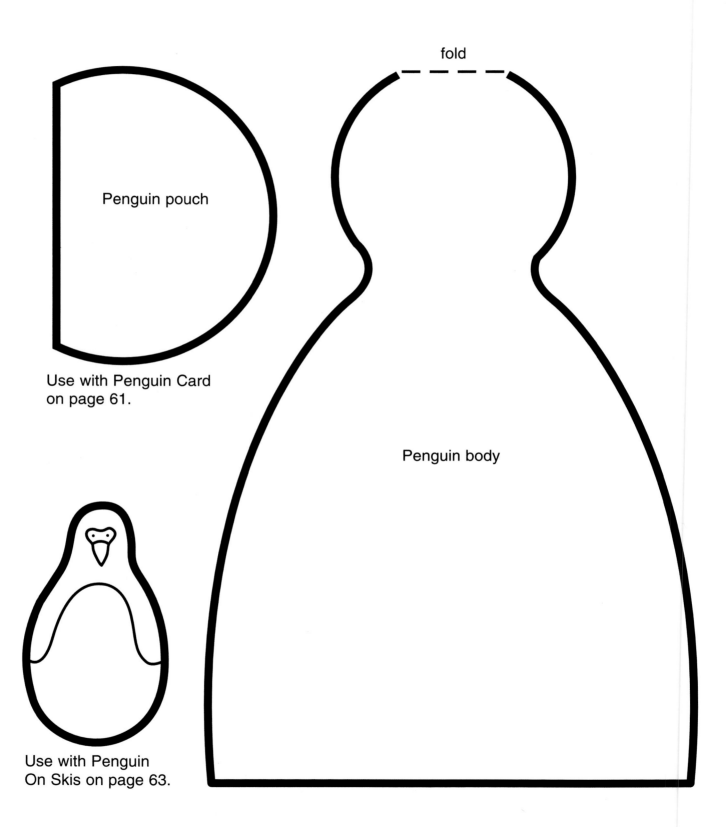

Penguin pouch

Use with Penguin Card
on page 61.

fold

Penguin body

Use with Penguin
On Skis on page 63.

Penguin On Skis

Materials For Each Child:

1 construction-paper penguin cutout
1 small cardboard carton, covered
   in blue construction paper
2 craft sticks
cotton balls and tagboard,
   or a cookie sheet covered
   with aluminum foil
black and orange markers
glue

Class Preparations:

Duplicate the pattern on page 62 on white construction paper and cut out for each child. Cover each carton in blue construction paper.

Directions:

1. Use markers to color the penguin's head and wings black. Color the beak orange.
2. Glue the penguin to the front of the carton.
3. Glue craft sticks to the bottom of the carton for skis, as shown.
4. Glue cotton balls to a sheet of tagboard to make a snow scene for displaying your penguin, or cover a cookie sheet with aluminum foil and have several penguins slide on the ice.

Arctic Animals

Materials For Each Child:

3 tagboard Arctic animal cutouts
1 sheet of 9" x 12" blue construction paper
white tempera paint in a shallow container
toothbrush

Class Preparations:

Use the patterns on page 64 to cut three Arctic animals from tagboard for each child. Pour paint into shallow containers. Cover work surfaces with newspaper.

Directions:

1. Arrange cutouts on a sheet of blue construction paper.
2. Lightly dip a toothbrush into white paint.
3. Holding the toothbrush over the paper, brush your thumb along the bristles to splatter paint a snowy effect. Allow the paint to dry.
4. Carefully remove the animal cutouts to reveal a snowy animal scene. 🅗

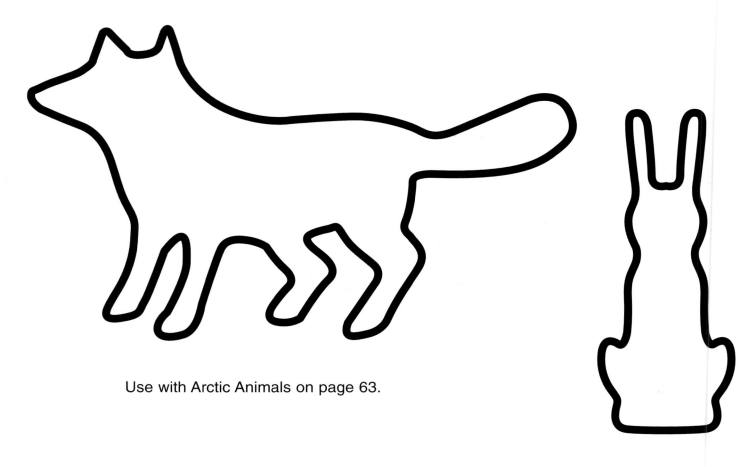

Use with Arctic Animals on page 63.

Snowstorm

Materials For Each Child:
1 white plastic bag, cut into tiny pieces
1 plastic screw-top jar
1 plastic toy, glued inside a plastic jar lid
water
glitter

Class Preparations:
For each child, cut a white plastic bag into tiny pieces. Use a hot-glue gun to glue each child's toy to the inside of a jar lid.

Directions:
1. Fill a jar with water and put a handful of plastic scraps and glitter into it.
2. Put the lid on in the normal way, screwing it on tightly. ⊕
3. Turn the jar upside down to make the snow fall.

Christmas Thank You

Materials For Each Child:
1 sheet of letter-writing paper
1 envelope
brown tempera paint in a shallow container
red and black fine-tip markers

Directions:
1. Dip your thumb in brown tempera paint. Make a thumbprint for a reindeer's body on the corner of a sheet of paper and on the corner of an envelope, as shown.
2. Dip the end of your little finger in brown tempera paint. Make a fingerprint for the reindeer's head next to each thumbprint. Allow the paint to dry.
3. Use markers to give each reindeer a red nose, black eyes, and a mouth, legs, and antlers, as shown.
4. Use the stationery for sending a Christmas message, a letter to Santa, or a thank-you letter.

Snow Scene

Materials For Each Child:

1 sheet of 9" x 12" dark blue
  construction paper
bubble-wrap and posterboard print
  block, to share
2 giftwrap Christmas tree cutouts
white tempera paint in a shallow container
glue

Class Preparations:

Cut a square of bubble wrap, 3" x 3" and glue it to a similar-sized piece of posterboard to make a print block. Make several blocks for your class to share. Use the pattern below to cut two Christmas trees from used Christmas giftwrap for each child. Pour paint into shallow containers.

Directions:

1. Dip a print block in white paint and press down gently on the dark blue paper to print a snowstorm. Repeat this step until the paper is covered. Allow the paint to dry.

2. Glue two trees along the bottom edge of the paper.

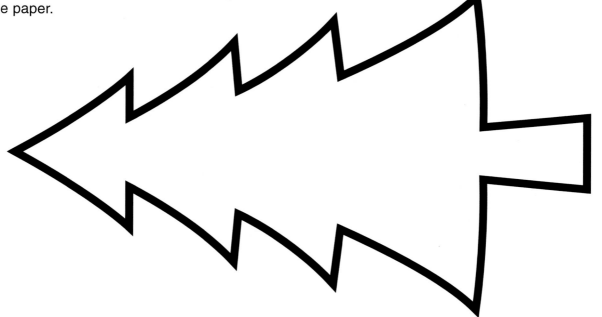

These simple-to-make musical instruments will help you start off the New Year with a bang!

Noisy Maracas

Materials For Each Child:

6 strips of crepe paper, 1" x 6"
2 paper plates, 10" in diameter
dried beans
tempera paints
paintbrushes
glue

Class Preparations:

For each child, cut six 1" x 6" crepe-paper strips.
Have a stapler ready.

Directions:

1. Paint patterns on the bottom of both plates.
2. Staple the plates together around the edge, leaving one small gap.
3. Pour a handful of dried beans into the gap.
4. Finish stapling the plates together.
5. Glue crepe-paper strips to the outside of the maraca, as shown.

New Year Noisemakers

Materials For Each Child:

2 paper cups
dry beans
colored paper strips
1 sticky label with the date of the New Year
glue

Class Preparations:

Cut different-colored paper scraps into strips. Write the date of the New Year on each child's sticky label. Have tape ready.

Directions:

1. Put some dry beans in one paper cup.
2. Tape the two paper cups together, as shown.
3. Decorate the outside of the cups by gluing on strips of colored paper.
4. Stick a date label on the noisemaker.
5. Rattle your noisemaker to welcome the New Year.

Valentine's Day is an opportunity to show your students the value of sharing and helping each other.

Join Hands

Materials For Each Child:
2 squares of colored construction paper, 6" x 6"
1 piece of yarn, 6" or 12" in length
black, white, and brown tempera paints in shallow trays
glue

Class Preparations:
For this group project, cut two squares of paper, 6" x 6", for each child. Have tape, scissors, and clothes hangers ready.

Directions:
1. Make one paint handprint on each piece of paper. Allow the paint to dry.
2. Swap one of your handprints with someone else.
3. Align and glue the two hands back to back. Allow the glue to dry.
4. Cut around the hand shape, leaving a generous outline, as shown.
5. Tape a length of yarn to the hands.
6. Tie your pair of hands onto a clothes hanger with several other pairs. 🅣

Wear A Heart

Materials For Each Child:
red tagboard heart cutout
glitter
sequins
glue in a tube

Class Preparations:
Use the pattern on the opposite page to cut a tagboard heart for each child. Have double-sided sticky tape ready.

Directions:
1. Squeeze glue onto the heart in a pattern and sprinkle on glitter.
2. Dot glue on the heart and press on sequins.
3. Leave to dry overnight.
4. Press a piece of double-sided sticky tape to the back so you can wear your heart. 🅗

I Love You!

. . . .

Materials For Each Child:
1 tagboard heart frame
1 sheet of 9" x 12" tagboard
fabric scraps
glue

Class Preparations:
Trace the heart pattern below onto
a sheet of tagboard for each child.
Cut out the heart to leave a frame.

Directions:
1. Glue fabric scraps onto a piece of
tagboard to make a patchwork design.
2. Glue the heart frame over the
top of the fabric design
to frame it.

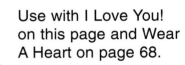

Use with I Love You!
on this page and Wear
A Heart on page 68.

Pink Cherry Blossoms

Materials For Each Child:
10 green construction-paper leaf cutouts
1 sheet of 9" x 12" white construction paper
popcorn and straw
red and white tempera paints
brown tempera paint in a shallow tray
paintbrushes
glue

Class Preparations:
Use the pattern on page 73 to cut out about
ten leaves from green construction paper for
each child. Pour brown paint into shallow trays.

Directions:
1. Mix together red and white paint to make
pink. Paint some popcorn pink and allow it to dry.
2. Paint a brown tree trunk on a sheet of white
construction paper.
3. Dip the side of a straw in brown paint. Use
it to print the tree's branches. Allow paint to dry.
4. Glue green paper leaves to the branches.
5. Glue popcorn onto the tree to make cherry
blossom. Add popcorn to the bottom of the
picture too for fallen blossoms.

Guess Who?

Materials For Each Child:
1 construction-paper card, 6" x 6"
2 red pipe cleaners
glitter and rice
glue

Class Preparations:
For each child, cut a 6" x 12" piece of
construction paper. Fold it in half to make
a square card, 6" x 6".

Directions:
1. Bend two pipe cleaners to make a heart,
as shown. Ⓗ
2. Glue the heart to the front of the card. Ⓗ
3. Spread glue inside the heart and sprinkle
on glitter and rice. Allow to dry.

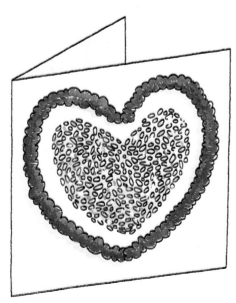

spring

Remember St. Patrick's Day on March 17th. Engage your class with fascinating Irish myths and legends.

Lucky Leprechaun Hat

Materials For Each Child:
1 green construction-paper circle cutout
15 green construction-paper leaf cutouts
gold foil or foil-covered chocolate coins
length of elastic and glue

Class Preparations:
Use the pattern on the opposite page to cut out a circle of light green construction paper, for each child. Make a cut from the outside to the center. Use the leaf pattern to cut out about 15 leaves for each child. Have tape and a pencil ready.

Directions:
1. Fold the paper circle into a cone and tape the cut ends in place. 🅗
2. Push a pencil through each side of the hat to make a hole. Thread elastic through and tie a knot in each end, to hold the hat on. 🅣
3. Glue paper leaves on your hat.
4. Crumple pieces of gold foil and flatten them to make coin shapes, or use chocolate coins. Glue the coins among the leaves.

Shamrock Pots

Materials For Each Child:
3 light green construction-paper hearts
1 strip of green crepe paper, 2" x 18"
yogurt container
craft stick
green glitter or sequins
modeling clay
glue

Class Preparations:
Use the pattern on the opposite page to cut three construction-paper hearts for each child. Cut strips of crepe paper measuring 2" x 18".

Directions:
1. Glue the hearts on the craft stick to make a shamrock, as shown.
2. Decorate the shamrock by gluing on green glitter or sequins.
3. Put a piece of modeling clay into the bottom of a yogurt container; then push the craft stick into the clay so that the shamrock stands up.
4. Tie a strip of green crepe paper in a bow around the container. 🅣

Use with Pink Cherry
Blossoms on page 70,
Lucky Leprechaun Hat
on page 72, and Summer
Bonnet on page 116.

Use with Shamrock
Pots on page 72.

Use with Lucky Leprechaun Hat on page 72,
Mexican Wall Mask on page 105, Bzzzzz! on
page 112, Balloon Ride on page 144, and
Piggy Face on page 150.

Leprechaun Mushrooms

Materials For Each Child:
1/4 sheet of 9" x 12" blue construction paper
1/4 apple
1/2 straw
a building block
several small paper circles
red, white, and green tempera paints
   in shallow containers
glitter and glue

Class Preparations:
Cut the apples into quarters and cut the straws in half. Make paper circles with a hole puncher. Cut a piece of 4½" x 6" blue construction paper for each child.

Directions:
1. To print the top of the mushroom, dip the flat side of the piece of apple in red paint and press on the paper.
2. Print a white stalk under the mushroom using a building block.
3. Print green grass around the bottom of the mushroom with the side of a straw. Allow to dry.
4. Glue on the paper circles to make spots on the mushroom.
5. Spread glue around the mushroom cap and sprinkle with glitter. Allow to dry.

It's Raining!

Materials For Each Child:
1 sheet of 9" x 12" light blue construction paper
1 construction-paper umbrella cutout
½ straw
plastic bag, cut into strips
brightly colored tempera paints
   in shallow containers
paintbrushes and glue

Class Preparations:
Use the pattern on page 76 to cut an umbrella from construction paper, for each child. Cut straws in half and old plastic bags into strips, one bag for each child.

Directions:
1. Dip the side of the straw in blue paint and use it to print slanted lines on the paper to look like pouring rain. Allow to dry.
2. Paint the handle of the umbrella cutout.
3. Glue the plastic strips on the top part of the umbrella, overlapping as shown. Allow to dry.
4. Glue the umbrella to the rainy background.

Brighten up a rainy spring day with colorful projects about weather.

Cloudy Day

Materials For Each Child:
1 sheet of 9" x 12" blue construction paper
container, larger than 9" x 12", filled with water
newspaper
pale gray tempera paint in a shallow container
sponge
wax crayons

Class Preparations:
Fill the large container with water.
Pour the paint into shallow containers.

Directions:
1. Use wax crayons to draw a springtime scene on the sheet of paper. You could include blossoms on trees, spring flowers, and baby rabbits. Do not draw anything on the sky.
2. Wet the sheet of paper by dipping the whole sheet into water.
3. Lay the wet paper flat on the newspaper.
4. Dip the sponge in the paint and dab it on the sheet of paper to make clouds. Watch as the color spreads over the picture.

Sun, Rain, Rainbow

Materials For Each Child:
1 sheet of 9" x 12" light yellow construction paper
1 yellow construction-paper circle cutout
uncooked rice
rainbow-colored tempera paints
paintbrushes and glue

Class Preparations:
Use a jar or round lid, 2"–3" in diameter, as a template to cut out a circle from yellow paper for each child.

Directions:
1. Paint a large rainbow in lots of colors on the paper, as shown.
2. Glue on the yellow circle for the sun, and paint yellow rays coming from it. Allow to dry.
3. Dot glue over the picture and sprinkle on grains of rice to make raindrops.
4. Allow to dry; then shake off excess rice.

Use with It's Raining! on page 74.

Splash!

Materials For Each Child:
1 white posterboard splash cutout
1 red posterboard boot cutout
foil or clear plastic
Styrofoam® balls, 1" in diameter
pipe cleaners and glitter
black marker, glue, and paintbrush

Class Preparations:
Use the pattern on page 78 to cut a red posterboard boot, for each child. Also, cut a splash shape, larger than the boot from white posterboard. Make small holes in the Styrofoam® balls. Have a hole puncher and tape ready.

Directions:
1. Spread glue over the splash cutout and cover with foil or clear plastic. Make wiggly lines of glue with a paintbrush and sprinkle on glitter.
2. Use a hole puncher to punch holes in the edge of the splash cutout. ⓣ
3. Use a black marker to draw the heel and sole on the bottom edge of the boot, as shown.
4. Glue the boot to the splash shape.
5. Spread glue on the Styrofoam® balls and pipe cleaners. Roll them in glitter; then allow to dry.
6. Stick the pipe cleaners into the Styrofoam® balls. Push each pipe cleaner through a hole in the splash shape and tape on the back. ⓗ

Rainbow Colors

Materials For Each Child:
1 sheet of 9" x 12" construction paper
1 container larger than 9" x 12", filled with water
rainbow-colored runny tempera paints
paintbrushes or spoons

Class Preparations:
Mix paint in rainbow colors—violet, indigo, blue, green, yellow, orange, and red—to a very runny consistency. Fill the large container with water.

Directions:
1. Dip the paper in the water.
2. Starting with violet, drip the runny paint from a paintbrush or spoon onto the wet paper in a small arc shape.
3. Take a different paintbrush or spoon and drip an indigo arc above the violet one.
4. Continue until you have painted the whole rainbow.

Use with Splash! on page 77.

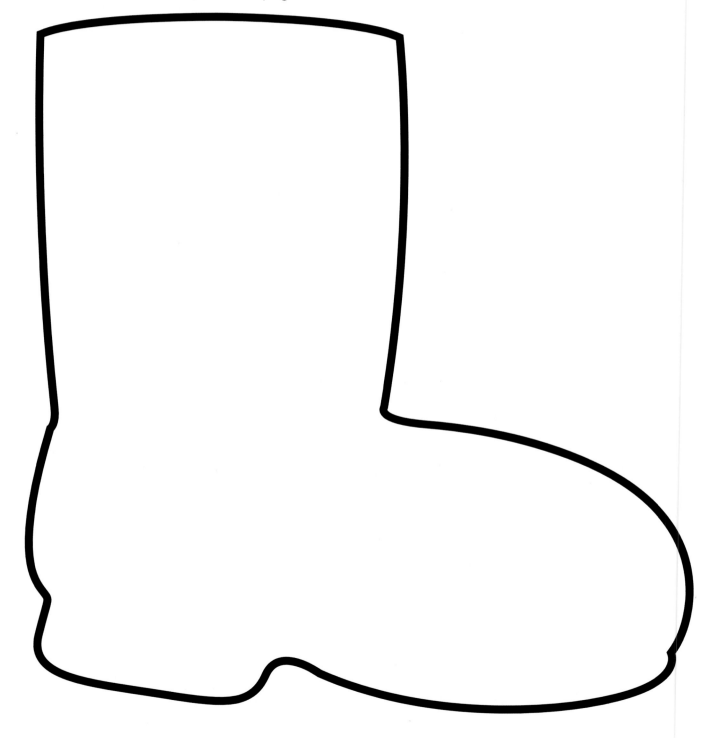

Lions and Lambs

Materials For Each Child:

1 cardboard tube
1 yellow tagboard lion cutout
1 white tagboard lamb cutout
shredded yellow paper
cotton balls
yellow tempera paint
paintbrush
glue

Class Preparations:

Duplicate the lion pattern below on yellow tagboard and the lamb pattern on white tagboard, for each child. Cut out the shapes.

Directions:

1. Paint one half of a cardboard tube yellow for the lion's coat. Allow to dry.
2. Glue the cotton balls on the plain end for the lamb's wool; then glue on the lamb's head (A).
3. Glue the shredded paper around the yellow end of the tube for the lion's mane; then glue on the lion's head, as shown.

Lamb

Lion

Wash Day

Materials For Each Child:
construction-paper clothes cutouts
small buttons
colored fine-tip markers
glue

Class Preparations:
For each child, enlarge by 200% and
duplicate the patterns on the opposite
page on white construction paper and
cut out. Have a length of string and
small clothespins or tape ready.

Directions:
1. Use markers to decorate the clothes with
your favorite colors.
2. Glue real buttons on your paper cutouts.
3. String a line across the classroom and hang
up the clothes using clothespins or tape. **T**

Wind Chimes

Materials For Each Child:
1 colored plastic cup with a hole in the base
4 different lengths of string, plus a long length
 to hang wind chimes
4 small bells

Class Preparations:
Make a hole in the base of each plastic
cup. Tie a large knot at the end of each
long length of string. Have tape ready.

Directions:
1. Thread the long piece of string through the
hole in the plastic cup so the knot is inside. **H**
2. Thread a bell onto a short length of string.
Pull the string through so that the bell is in the
middle of the string.
3. Tape both ends of the string to the inside
of the cup. **H**
4. Repeat steps 2 and 3 with three
more bells. **H**
5. Hang the wind chimes outside your
classroom and hear them tinkle in the breeze. **T**

spring

Use with Wash Day on page 80.

Spring Windows

1 piece of 8" x 18" waxed paper
1 tissue-paper flower, egg, and bunny
glue

Class Preparations:
Use the patterns on page 84 to cut one
tissue-paper flower, one egg, and one bunny
for each child. Cut a piece of 8" x 18" waxed
paper for each child. Have tape ready.

Directions:
1. Fold the waxed paper in half lengthwise.
2. Open the paper out flat; then spread glue on
one side. Carefully lay the tissue-paper shapes
on the glued side.
3. Fold the waxed paper over carefully to
sandwich the tissue-paper shapes. Allow to dry.
4. Tape the artwork to the classroom window,
so that the sun can shine
through. ⓣ

High In The Sky

Materials For Each Child:
1 construction-paper kite cutout
1 piece of drinking straw, 10" in length
1 piece of drinking straw, 6" in length
6 strips of 1" x 3" fabric
a long length of string
tempera paints
paintbrushes and glue

Class Preparations:
Use the pattern on the opposite page
to cut a kite shape for each child, from
construction paper. Also, cut six fabric
strips and two different lengths of drinking
straw for each child. Have tape ready.

Directions:
1. Paint the kite your favorite color and
allow to dry.
2. Glue lengths of straw in a cross from corner
to corner as shown.
3. Tie the strips of fabric along the string. ⓗ
4. Tape one end of the string to
the kite, as shown. ⓗ

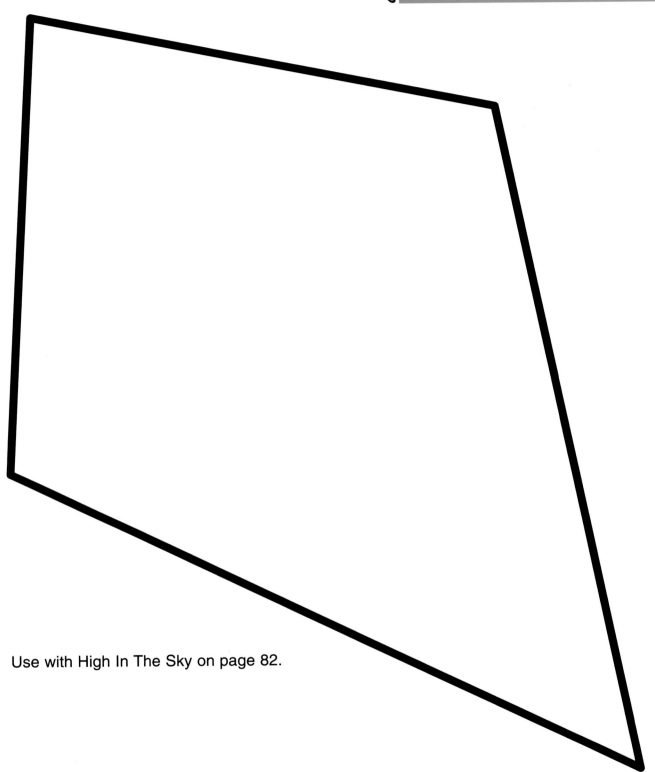

Use with High In The Sky on page 82.

Use with Spring Windows on page 82 and Peek-A-Boo Bunny on page 100.

Trees and flowers are springing to life outside. Create an indoor garden and watch new shoots grow.

Watch It Grow!

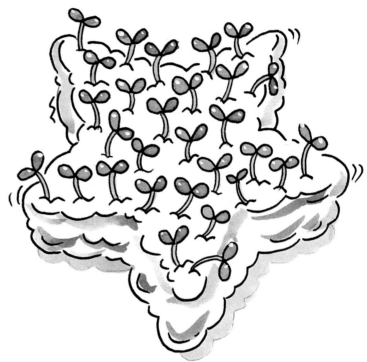

Materials For Each Child:
cookie cutter
cookie sheet
cotton
alfalfa sprout seeds and water

Directions:
1. Lay the cookie cutter on the cookie sheet and push cotton into the shape, making sure to fill in all the corners. ⓗ
2. Pour water onto the cotton until it is thoroughly soaked.
3. Sprinkle a thin layer of alfalfa sprout seeds onto the cotton.
4. Place the cookie sheet in a sunny spot. After a few days, remove the cookie cutter carefully. Keep the cotton moist and watch the sprouts grow!

Mystery Garden

Materials For Each Child:
plastic container with holes in the bottom
colored construction-paper shapes
potting soil and water
plastic lid
mixed birdseed
craft stick
glue

Class Preparations:
Cut colored construction paper into decorative shapes. Use sharp scissors to poke holes in the bottom of each child's plastic container.

Directions:
1. Glue colored construction-paper shapes on the outside of your container to decorate it.
2. Fill the container with soil reaching to about 1/2" from the top.

3. Set the container on the lid, then water the soil.
4. Sprinkle on birdseed.
5. Write your name on the craft stick and push into the soil. ⓗ
6. Put the container on a windowsill and keep moist.
7. Wait and see what grows.

Before you do this project, explain to your students how a tiny acorn can grow into a towering oak tree.

Big Acorn Card

● ●

Materials For Each Child:
1 sheet of folded 9" x 12" white
 construction paper
strips of brown paper, about 1" wide
green paper scraps
light brown construction-paper nut cutout
green construction-paper cap cutout
colored pencils
glue

Class Preparations:
Use the patterns on the right to cut out a nut from light brown construction paper and a cap from green construction paper for each child. Fold sheets of white construction paper in from both sides so that the edges meet in the middle. Cut strips of brown paper, about 1" wide, for children to share.

Directions:
1. Glue strips of brown paper inside the card to make the trunk and branches of an oak tree.
2. Tear green paper scraps into small pieces. Glue them to the branches of the tree for leaves.
3. Use colored pencils to draw patterns on the acorn cap, as shown.
4. Glue the nut to one side of the card and the cap to the other. When the card is closed, a whole acorn shows. When it is open, the oak tree that grows from the acorn can be seen.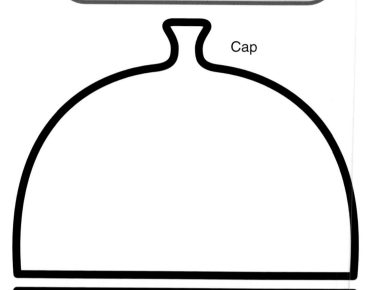

Cap

Nut

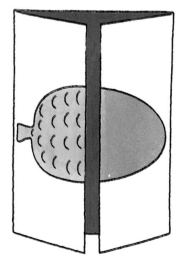

spring

> Make your classroom festive with multi-colored eggs. The Easter holiday is on its way!

Spring Blossom

Materials For Each Child:
1 twig with several tips
1 yogurt container
modeling clay in pink, yellow, white, and green
sand or pebbles

Directions:
1. Roll balls of pink, yellow, and white modeling clay to make blossoms about the size of peas.
2. Push the balls onto the tips of the twigs.
3. Make leaves by rolling small balls of green clay, flattening them, then folding them around the twig.
4. Fill a yogurt container with sand or pebbles and push your blossoming twig into it.

Broken Eggs

Materials For Each Child:
1 tagboard egg cutout
tempera paints
paintbrushes
colored fine-tip markers
  or colored crayons

Class Preparations:
Use the pattern on page 88 to cut an egg from tagboard for each child. Have pinking shears and tape ready.

Directions:
1. Decorate your egg cutout with paint, fine-tip markers, or colored crayons.
2. Use pinking shears to cut the egg in half in a zigzag. 🅣
3. Tape your two egg halves to the classroom window. 🅣

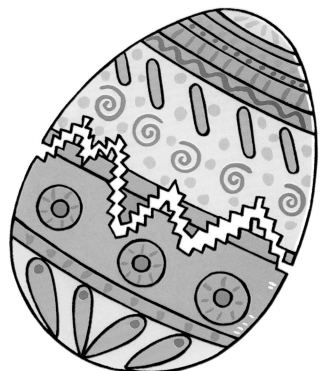

87

Use with Broken Eggs on page 87.

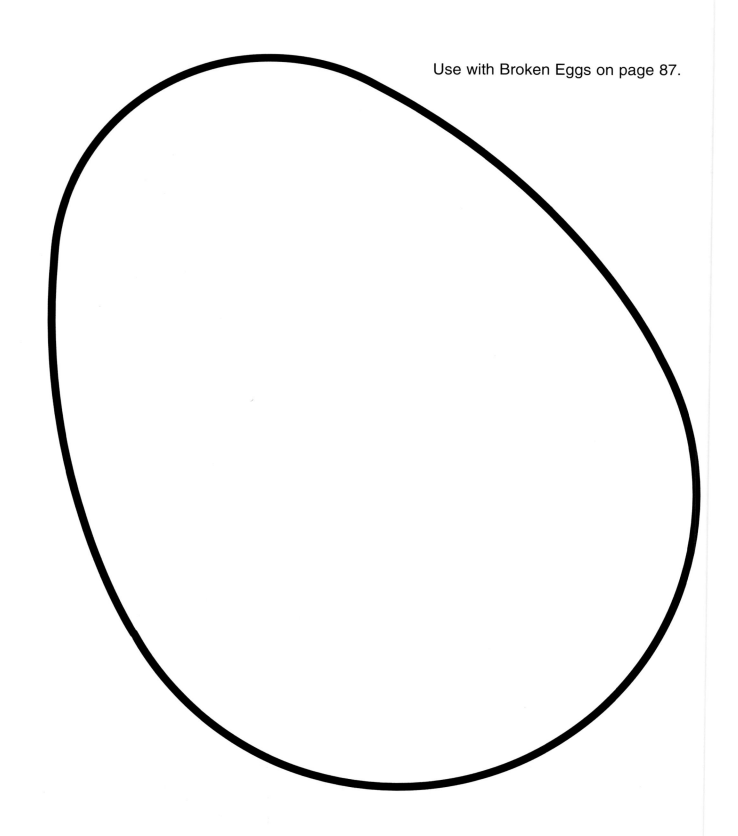

Easter Egg Tree

Materials For Each Child:
self-hardening, colored modeling clay
pencil
plastic fork
ruler
thread

Class Preparations:
For this group project, stand a branch in a flowerpot. Anchor with pebbles to make a class tree.

Directions:
1. Mold the clay into an egg shape.
2. Press the shape down on the table to flatten it.
3. Make patterns on the surface of the egg by pressing in the end of a pencil, plastic fork, or side of a ruler.
4. Poke a hole in the top with a pencil for hanging. Leave the egg to harden overnight. ⒣
5. Insert thread through the hole in the egg and tie to make a loop. Hang an egg on each branch of the class tree. ⓣ

Build A Nest

Materials For Each Child:
1 paper plate, 10" in diameter
scraps such as long and short lengths of string, yarn, raffia, pipe cleaners, shredded paper, and small pieces of aluminum foil
chocolate eggs in foil
glue

Directions:
1. Spread glue around the edge of a plate.
2. Press on scraps to build up a nest around the plate, adding more glue when necessary.
3. When the glue is dry, place chocolate eggs in the center of the nest.

Splatter Egg

• • • • • • • • • • • • • • • • •

Materials For Each Child:
1 hard-boiled egg
newspaper
dry pasta
tempera paints
paintbrushes
glue

Class Preparations:
For each child, boil one egg for ten minutes; then allow to cool.

Directions:
1. Paint the egg all over in one color. Allow to dry for about ten minutes.
2. Spread newspaper on the floor and place the egg on it.
3. Dip a brush into a different-colored paint and flick at the egg to splatter on paint. Allow to dry.
4. Turn the egg over on a clean sheet of newspaper and flick paint on the other side.
5. Glue small pasta shapes together to make a nest. Display your egg on the pasta nest, but don't eat it!

Eggs In A Nest

• • • • • • • • • • • • • • • • • •

Materials For Each Child:
cornstarch clay in different colors

Class Preparations:
Use the recipe on page 5 to make up batches of cornstarch clay. Create different colors by adding different food coloring to it.

Directions:
1. Roll brown clay into very thin, long sausage shapes to make twigs. Ⓗ
2. Arrange the clay twigs to make a nest.
3. Make two thick, long sausages of different-colored clay. Lay one next to the other; then roll them up and knead until smooth. The clay will have a marbled pattern.
4. Divide the marbled clay and mold into egg shapes; then display them in the nest.

Eggshell Cards

Materials For Each Child:
pieces of different-colored broken eggshell,
   in separate dishes
1 construction-paper egg card
pencil and glue

Class Preparations:
You will need about one egg per child. Boil the
eggs for ten minutes in water with a few drops of
food coloring. Make several batches in different
colors. Allow the eggs to cool; then remove the
shells and break them into pieces. Place each
color in a different dish. To make a card, fold a
sheet of 9" x 12" construction paper in half.
Then use the pattern below to draw an egg
against the fold. Cut out the egg, but do not
cut along the fold.

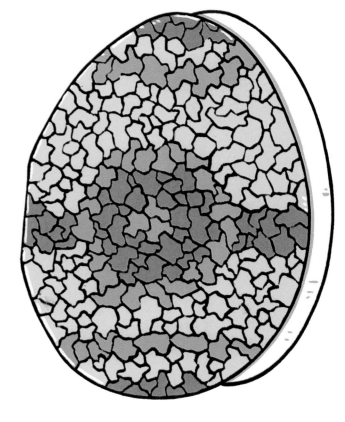

Directions:
1. Draw a pattern or picture on the card.
2. Spread glue all over the front of the card.
3. Stick on pieces of different-colored
eggshell to fill in the pattern or
picture. Press down on each piece
to break it into tiny fragments.
Allow to dry.
4. Write a message to a
friend inside the card. ⓣ

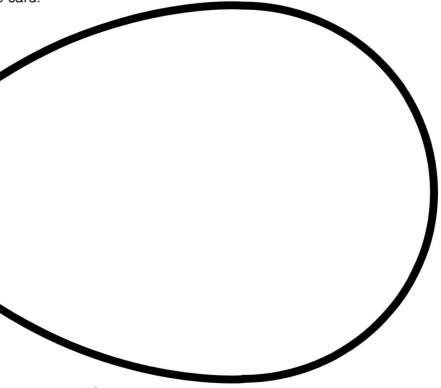

Use with Eggshell
Cards on this page
and Hide-And-Seek
Card on page 92.

Fly Away

Materials For Each Child:
1 tagboard bird body and 2 tagboard wings
2 wiggle eyes
1 brass fastener
2 feathers
a length of narrow ribbon
tempera paints and paintbrushes
glue

Class Preparations:
Use the pattern on the opposite page to cut out a tagboard bird body and two wings for each child. Have tape ready.

Directions:
1. Paint some patterns on one side of the bird body and wings. Allow to dry, then paint the other sides. Allow to dry.
2. Glue feathers on the bird to make a tail.
3. Glue on wiggle eyes.
4. Place a wing on each side of the body and push a brass fastener through to secure. (T)
5. Tape a piece of ribbon to the bird's back to hang it up. (H)

Hide-And-Seek Card

Materials For Each Child:
1 sheet of 9" x 12" colored construction paper, cut in two pieces, one with egg outline
white tempera paint and paintbrush
chenille chick or chick sticker
glue

Class Preparations:
For each child, cut two rectangles from a sheet of construction paper. Make one rectangle 4$\frac{1}{2}$" x 12" and the other 4$\frac{1}{2}$" x 10". Use the pattern on page 91 to draw a large egg on the longer piece of construction paper. Have scissors ready.

Directions:
1. Paint the egg white.
2. Fold back each end of the paper with the egg painting to make a flap about 1" wide. (H)
3. Cut the egg in half in a zigzag. (T)
4. Glue a chenille chick or sticker in the middle of the smaller piece of construction paper.
5. Glue the flaps to the back of the smaller piece of paper, as shown. (H)

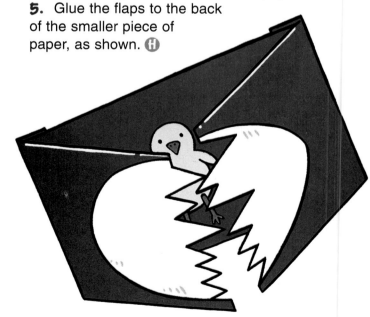

Use with Fly Away on page 92.

Yummy Worm

· ·

Materials For Each Child:

1 paper plate, 10" in diameter
several yellow construction-paper feather cutouts
1 orange construction-paper diamond
2 gummy worms
yellow tempera paint
paintbrush
black fine-tip marker
glue

Class Preparations:

Use the patterns below to cut out four or five
feathers from yellow construction paper and
a diamond from orange construction paper
for the beak for each child.

Directions:

1. Paint the plate yellow and allow to dry.
2. Glue paper feathers to the back of the
plate, along the top edge.
3. Add eyes with a marker.
4. Fold the orange diamond in half and
glue one half to the plate to make a beak.
5. Glue a gummy worm under the chick's
beak. The extra gummy worm is for eating!

Easter Pets

• • • • • • • • • • • • • • • •

Materials For Each Child:
1 hard-boiled egg
1 screw-top from a soda bottle
1 cotton ball per bunny
1 piece of string, 4" in length per mouse
construction-paper scraps
black marker
glue

Class Preparations:
Hard boil an egg for each child and allow to
cool. Have the children decide whether they are
going to make a chick, a bunny, or a mouse. For
each chick, cut an orange comb, two round blue
eyes, and an orange triangle for the beak from
construction paper. For each bunny, cut two long
brown ovals for the ears, two round blue eyes, a
black triangle for the nose, a white square for
the teeth, and black strips for whiskers. You also
need a cotton ball for the tail. For each mouse,
cut two round brown ears, two round black eyes,
one black nose, and black strips for whiskers.
You also need a 4" length of string for the tail.

Directions:
1. To make a chick, glue the comb to the
bigger end of an egg. Glue on the eyes and
draw on black pupils, as shown. Glue on the
orange triangle for a beak.
2. To make a bunny, glue the ears to the
bigger end of an egg. Glue on the eyes, nose,
teeth, and whiskers. Draw pupils on the eyes
and a line down the square for two teeth, as
shown. Glue a cotton ball to the back of the
bunny to make a tail.
3. To make a mouse, glue the ears to the
bigger end of an egg. Glue on the eyes,
whiskers, and nose, as shown. Glue the tail
to the back of the mouse.
4. Balance your pet on an upturned bottle top
to display it, but don't eat the egg!

95

spring

The countryside is full of baby animals in springtime. Tell your class to keep an eye out for them!

Beaky Bookmark

Materials For Each Child:
1 brown construction-paper bookmark
black marker
2 wiggle eyes and glue

Class Preparations:
For each child, cut a rectangle of brown construction paper, about 2" x 6", to make a bookmark. Fold the bookmark in half, lengthwise. A third of the way down, cut an angled slit in the fold, about 1" in length to make a beak; then unfold the bookmark.

Directions:
1. Use a marker to draw feathers on your bookmark, as shown, to look like an owl.
2. Glue on two wiggle eyes.
3. Slot the owl's beak over a page in a book to mark your place.

Flappers

Materials For Each Child:
yellow tagboard cutouts of 1 hen and 1 hen wing or 1 chick and 2 chick wings
1 or 2 brass fasteners
modeling clay
straw or yellow shredded paper
craft stick
orange fine-tip marker
glue

Class Preparations:
Use the patterns on the opposite page to cut out a yellow tagboard bird shape—a hen or a chick—and matching wings for each child. Use a hole puncher to punch holes in the sides of the bodies and in the wings, as shown.

Directions:
1. Use a marker to draw a beak on the bird cutout. Glue on wiggle eyes.
2. Attach the wings with brass fasteners. 🄗
3. Glue a craft stick to the back of your bird.
4. Put modeling clay along the classroom windowsill and cover it with a layer of straw or yellow shredded paper. 🅣
5. Push your craft stick into the clay so that your bird stands up.

96

Use with Flappers on page 96.

Hen

Hen wing

Chick

Chick wing

Chirpees

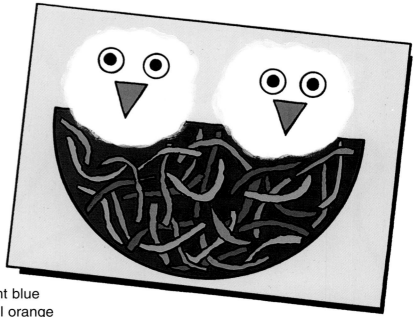

Materials For Each Child:
1/2 sheet of 9" x 12" light blue
   construction paper
1 brown construction-paper nest cutout
2 orange construction-paper triangles
2 white cotton balls
4 wiggle eyes
shredded wheat cereal
glue

Class Preparations:
For each child, cut a piece of 9" x 6" light blue
construction paper and cut out two small orange
construction-paper triangles. Use the pattern
on page 40 to cut out a semicircular nest from
brown construction paper.

Directions:
1. Glue the nest on the light blue paper near
the bottom edge.
2. Glue two cotton balls along the straight
edge of the nest, as shown.
3. Glue a pair of wiggle eyes and an orange
beak on each cotton ball.
4. Spread glue on the nest and sprinkle on
shredded wheat cereal. Allow to dry.

Spring Lambs

Materials For Each Child:
1/2 sheet of 9" x 12" black construction paper
1 wiggle eye
a colorful narrow ribbon, tied in a small bow
cotton balls
pencil and glue

Class Preparations:
For each child, make a small bow from
ribbon and cut a piece of 9" x 6" black
construction paper. Have scissors ready.

Directions:
1. Trace around your hand on black paper.
2. Cut out the shape. ⓣ
3. Glue a wiggle eye on the thumb part of the
cutout, to make a face.
4. Glue on cotton balls to cover the body.
5. Glue a colorful bow on your lamb.

Rainbow Rabbit

Materials For Each Child:
1 sheet of 9" x 12" black construction paper,
   with rabbit outline
tempera paints in shallow dishes
Q-Tips®

Class Preparations:
Use the pattern below to trace a rabbit
outline on each child's paper. Use chalk
so that it can be rubbed off later.

Directions:
1. Use Q-Tips® dipped in paint to print tiny
dots inside the rabbit outline. Use a different
Q-Tip® for each color.
2. Dip a Q-Tip® in black paint and use
it to print an eye and a nose.
3. When the paint is dry, rub off the
chalk outline.

Peek-A-Boo Bunny

Materials For Each Child:
1 gray construction-paper bunny cutout
1 sheet of 9" x 12" light blue construction paper
1 sheet of 9" x 12" green construction paper
black fine-tip marker
glue

Class Preparations:
Use the pattern on page 84 to cut a gray construction-paper bunny for each child.

Directions:
1. Glue the bunny on the light blue paper.
2. Use a marker to draw eyes, a nose, and whiskers on your bunny.
3. Tear green construction paper into strips.
4. Glue strips in front of the bunny to make a grassy field.

Funny Bunnies

Materials For Each Child:
2–3 sheets of 9" x 12" construction paper
pink tempera paint and paintbrush
fine-tip markers

Directions:
1. Paint the palm of your hand and your index and fourth finger.
2. Press your hand down onto the paper, taking care not to let it slip. (It may take a few tries to make a really good bunny head print.)
3. Allow to dry.
4. Add eyes, nose, mouth, teeth, and whiskers with markers.

Hand-made jewelry makes a unique and special Mother's Day gift. Try these original ideas.

A Gold Star For Mom

Materials For Each Child:
cornstarch clay, about the size of a tennis ball
a paper clip
a long length of ribbon
rolling pins to share
cookie cutters to share
gold tempera paint
paintbrush
gold glitter
glue

Class Preparations:
Use the recipe on page 5 to make up a batch of cornstarch clay.

Directions:
1. Use a rolling pin to roll out the clay. Cut out a star using a cookie cutter.
2. Push a paper clip into one of the star's points. Allow to dry overnight.
3. When the clay is dry, paint a pattern on it with the gold paint. Allow to dry.
4. Spread glue in a pattern on the star and sprinkle on gold glitter. Allow to dry.
5. Thread ribbon through the paper clip and give to Mom.

Recycled Plastic Bag Bracelet

Materials For Each Child:
1 bracelet cut from a plastic bottle, 1½" wide
5 colorful plastic strips

Class Preparations:
For each child, use a craft knife to cut a bracelet, 1½" wide, from a plastic bottle. Cut colorful plastic bags into long strips, approximately 2" wide. Have tape ready.

Directions:
1. Tape one end of a plastic strip to the inside of the bracelet. Ⓣ
2. Wind the strip around the bracelet, leaving a gap between each loop.
3. Tape the end and start again with a strip of a different color, filling in the gaps as you go. Ⓣ
4. Continue until the bracelet is completely covered and well padded.

Bold Batik

• • • • • • • • • • • •

Materials For Each Child:
flour-and-water paste in an empty
   dish-detergent bottle
1 square of cotton fabric, 12" x 12"
fabric paints and paintbrushes

Class Preparations:
For each child, mix flour and water together
to make a smooth, fairly thick paste. Put it
in an empty dish-detergent bottle, ready for
immediate use. Cut a square of cotton
fabric, 12" x 12" for each child.

Directions:
1. Squeeze the paste out of the bottle
onto the fabric to make a pattern. Allow
to dry overnight.
2. Paint all over the dry, glued fabric
with fabric paint. Allow to dry overnight.
3. Peel off the paste to see the pattern.

Pasta Pendant

• • • • • • • • • • • • • •

Materials For Each Child:
1 tagboard disk, 3" in diameter
dry pasta shapes
a long length of cord
tempera paint
paintbrush
glitter glue
glue

Class Preparations:
Use a jar lid, 3" in diameter, as a template
to cut a tagboard disk for each child.
Use a hole puncher to make a hole near
the edge of each disk.

Directions:
1. Paint the disk a bright color. Allow to dry.
2. Glue on pasta shapes to make
a pattern. Allow to dry.
3. Add glitter glue or more paint as
a finishing touch.
4. Thread a length of cord through the
finished disk to make a pendant. Ⓗ

Have your youngsters surprise Dad on Father's Day by giving him a framed self-portrait!

Sew A Picture Frame

Materials For Each Child:
1 colored tagboard frame, 9" x 12"
1 sheet of 9" x 12" tagboard
1 piece of colored cord, about 40" in length
a picture or photograph, about 5" x 7"
tempera paints and paintbrushes
glue

Class Preparations:
For each child, use a craft knife to cut a sheet of colored tagboard into a frame with borders about 2½" wide. Place the frame on another tagboard sheet and use a hole puncher to punch holes through them both, as shown. Have tape ready.

Directions:
1. Decorate the frame with paint.
2. Allow to dry; then glue the picture or photo in the center of the sheet of tagboard.
3. Spread glue around the edges of the sheet of tagboard. Press the frame on the sheet, being careful to line up the punched holes. Allow to dry. (H)
4. Thread cord through the holes. (H)
5. Tape the ends of the cord at the back.

Perfect Pencil Caddy Present

Materials For Each Child:
1 clean, plastic pint container
a piece of construction paper to fit around container
magazine scraps or stickers
tempera paints and paintbrushes
a length of ribbon and glue

Class Preparations:
Ask your class to collect pint containers from frozen yogurt or ice-cream. Cut a piece of construction paper to fit around each container.

Directions:
1. Wrap the paper around the container and glue. (H)
2. Paint on designs or glue on pictures from magazines. (Use stickers if desired.)
3. Wrap the ribbon around the caddy and tie in a bow. (T)

Notes For Dad

Materials For Each Child:
1 tagboard car or truck cutout
1 index card with message
1 clothespin
fine-tip markers in various colors
glue

Class Preparations:
Use the patterns below to cut out a tagboard car or truck for each child. Have each child dictate a message as you write on an index card.

Directions:
1. Decorate one side of the cutout with markers.
2. Label the cutout, as shown. 🅣
3. Glue the cutout to a clothespin, leaving the top of the pin poking up as shown.
4. Clip the index card to the pin and give to Dad to hold notes.

Discuss with your students the Mexican holiday of Cinco de Mayo. Then re-create a masked parade!

Mexican Wall Mask

Materials For Each Child:
1 posterboard mask
1 colored construction-paper rectangle
craft stick
lengths of drinking straws
colored markers
masking tape
glue

Class Preparations:
Use the template on page 73 to cut out a large posterboard circle for each child. Use a craft knife to cut out the eyes and nose. Cut straws into 3" lengths and cut a 2" x 4" colored construction-paper rectangle. Provide pictures of masks in reference books and have masking tape ready.

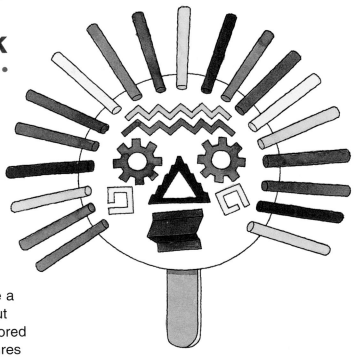

Directions:
1. Glue the straws around the edge of the mask, as shown.
2. Decorate around the eyes and nose with markers.
3. Bend and glue on a paper rectangle to form the mouth, as shown. 🖐
4. Tape the mask to a craft stick. 🖐

Pretty Place Mats

Materials For Each Child:
1 sheet of 9" x 12" blue construction paper
paper doily
tempera paints in shallow trays
sponges

Class Preparations:
Pour paints into shallow trays. Have clear Con-Tact® paper or laminating film ready.

Directions:
1. Lay the doily on the paper and sponge over the top of it with paints. Use a different sponge for each color. Be careful not to move the doily.
2. Lift up the doily carefully, and allow the paint to dry.
3. Put the doily in a different position on the paper, and sponge with paint again.
4. Repeat until the mat is painted. Allow to dry.
5. Cover the mat with clear Con-Tact® paper or laminating film. 🆃

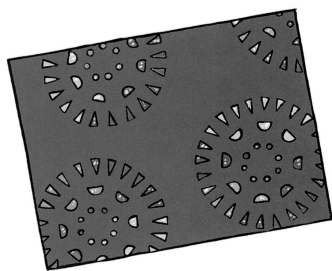

Cactus Garden

. . . .

Materials For Each Child:
1 posterboard cactus cutout
10 wooden toothpicks, cut in half
yellow tissue-paper scraps
a yogurt container filled with sand or pebbles
green tempera paint in shallow containers
sponge and glue

Class Preparations:
For each child, use the pattern below to cut a posterboard cactus. Cut ten toothpicks in half. Fill yogurt containers with sand or pebbles.

Directions:
1. Paint the cactus by dipping the sponge into paint and dabbing it on the cutout. Allow to dry.
2. Paint the other side to match. Allow to dry.
3. Glue the sides of the toothpicks on the cactus to make spikes on both sides.
4. Crumple yellow tissue-paper scraps to create cactus flowers. Glue onto the cactus tips.

5. Stand up the cactus in a yogurt container filled with sand or pebbles.
6. Place all of the cactus pots on a table to make a painted desert. ⓣ

Welcome warm, sunny days by turning your classroom into a glorious garden. Here's a bunch of lively ideas!

Summer Grass

Materials For Each Child:
4 colored construction-paper
    flower cutouts
4 craft sticks
aluminum foil tray
soil
grass seed
water and glue

Class Preparations:
Use the patterns on this page to cut four different-colored construction-paper flowers for each child. Fill the aluminum tray with soil.

Directions:
1. Glue the flowers to the craft sticks and allow to dry.
2. Water the soil and scatter grass seed on it.
3. Push the flower sticks into the soil in the tray.
4. Put the tray in a light place and continue to water; then wait for the grass to grow around the flowers.

Daisy Border

Materials For Each Child:
1/2 sheet of 9" x 12" green construction paper
1 leaf
gold glitter
white tempera paint in a shallow container
glue

Class Preparations:
For this group project, cut a sheet of 9" x 12" construction paper in half lengthwise for each child. You could cut the short ends at angles to make a curving border. Have some tape ready.

Directions:
1. Dip the leaf in the paint and use it to print the petals of a flower at one end of the paper.
2. Working along the paper, print more flowers until the paper is full. Allow to dry.
3. Put glue in the center of each flower and sprinkle on glitter. Allow to dry.
4. Join all the short edges of the sheets together with tape and make a border around the classroom. ⓣ

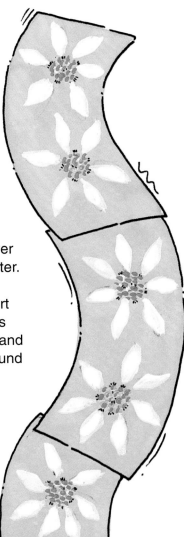

Sunny Sunflower

Materials For Each Child:
1 sheet of 9" x 12" construction paper
1 small, round aluminum-foil pie dish or jar lid
sunflower seeds
orange and black tempera paints in shallow containers
pencil and glue

Class Preparations:
Pour paint into containers.

Directions:
1. Dip the aluminum-foil pie dish or jar lid in orange paint and use it to print a circle on the paper for the center of the sunflower.
2. Glue sunflower seeds around the outside for petals.
3. To print seeds on the circle, dip the end of a pencil in black paint.

109

Garden Glove
Caterpillar Container

• •

Materials For Each Child:

1 oatmeal container or coffee can with lid
1 piece of green construction paper, large
   enough to wrap around container
1 green tagboard circle
1 green pipe cleaner cut in half
construction-paper scraps
black fine-tip marker
glue

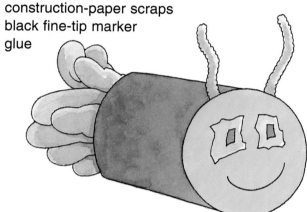

Class Preparations:

For each child, cut a circle of green tagboard
slightly larger than the diameter of the container.
Cut a piece of green construction paper to wrap
around the length of each child's container.
Cut green pipe cleaners in half for antennae.

Directions:

1. Glue the green construction paper around
the length of the container. Allow to dry. Ⓗ
2. For eyes, tear two construction-paper
squares and glue them on the green circle.
Then tear two smaller squares in a different
color and glue on top for pupils.
3. Glue two pieces of pipe cleaner to the back
of the green circle near the top for antennae.
Add a smile with a marker.
4. Glue the face to the bottom of the container.
5. Use the caterpillar container to store your
garden gloves.

Udderly Lovely

• •

Materials For Each Child:

1 sheet of 9" x 12" white
   construction-paper, with cow outline
black ink pads or thick black
   tempera paint in a shallow container
gray and black markers

Class Preparations:

For each child, duplicate the cow pattern on
the opposite page onto white construction paper.

Directions:

1. Use markers to color the cow's horns,
eyes, nostrils, hoofs, and tail.
2. Use black ink or thick paint to make
thumb-print patches on the cow.

Use with Udderly Lovely on page 110.

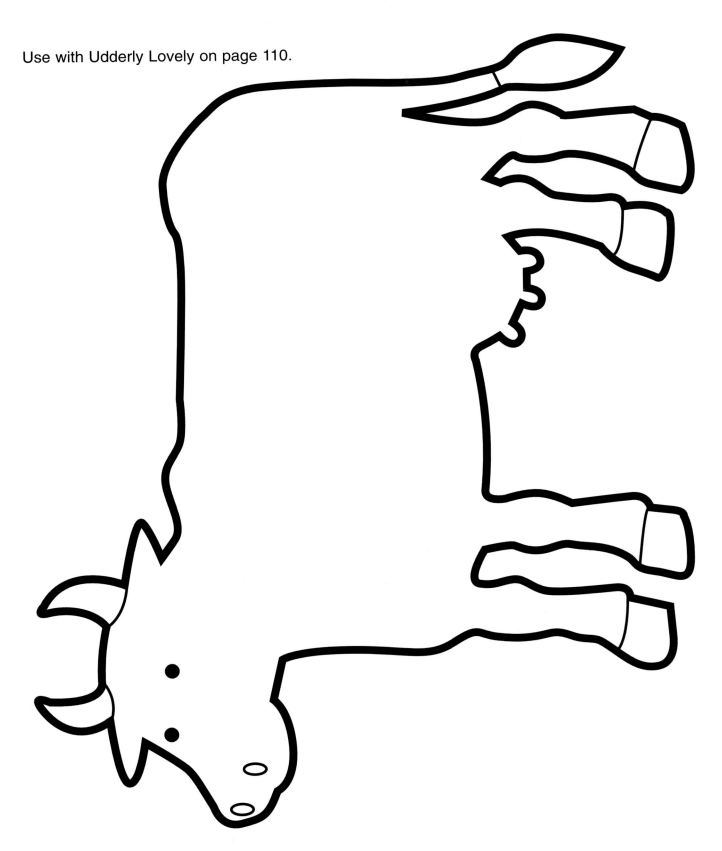

Have your students search outside for creepy crawlies; then make lots of busy bugs and bees.

Buzzin' Bees

Materials For Each Child:
1 sheet of 9" x 12" construction paper
tempera paints, including yellow, in containers
black and green fine-tip markers

Class Preparations:
Pour paint into containers.

Directions:
1. Use a marker to draw some long green stalks at the bottom of the paper.
2. Dip a finger into paint and print flower petals and centers at the top of each stalk.
3. Dip a finger into yellow paint and print bees buzzing around the flowers. Allow to dry.
4. Add stripes, wings, antennae, and eyes to the bees with a black fine-tip marker.

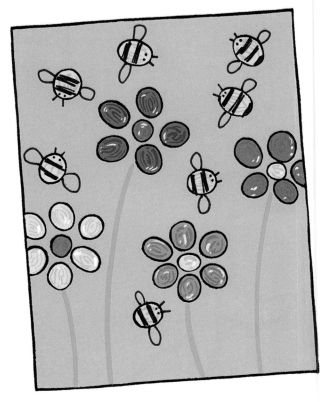

Bzzzzz!

Materials For Each Child:
1 brightly colored construction-paper
  flower cutout
1 yellow pompom
1 black pipe cleaner
2 wiggle eyes
glue

Class Preparations:
Use the pattern on page 73 to cut a circle from construction paper for each child. Cut petal shapes around the outside. Make a cut from the edge to the center. Have tape ready.

Directions:
1. Fold the paper flower into a cone shape and tape in place. 🅗
2. Wrap a pipe cleaner around the pompom to make a striped bee. Glue on two wiggle eyes.
3. Glue the bee to the inside of the flower.

Bug Garden

Materials For Each Child:
1 sheet 9" x 12" construction paper
tempera paints in saucers
black fine-tip marker

Class Preparations:
Pour paint into saucers.

Directions:
1. Curl up your little finger and dip the side of it into paint. Press onto the paper to print a snail's shell. Wash your hand.
2. Straighten out your finger and dip the side into a different-colored paint. Print a line under the snail's shell for the body, as shown.
3. Make butterflies and ladybugs using thumb and fingerprints, as shown.
4. When the paint is dry, use a marker to add antennae and other markings to the bugs.

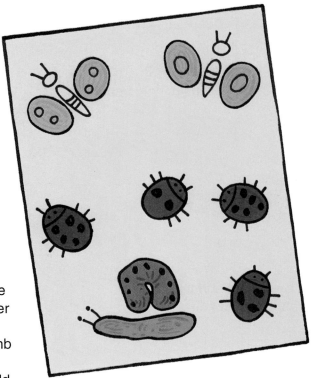

Summer Garden

Materials For Each Child:
3–5 squares of colored tissue paper, 4" x 4"
1 straw
brown non-hardening modeling clay and glue

Class Preparations:
For this group project, cut a class supply of tissue-paper squares.

Directions:
1. Twist squares of tissue paper together; then glue them at the twisted join to make flowers.
2. Push the flowers inside one end of a straw, as shown. Allow to dry.
3. Press modeling clay along the length of the classroom windowsill to make a flower bed.
4. Poke the end of the straw into the clay.

summer

Flowers and Butterflies

Materials For Each Child:
2 sheets of 9" x 12" white construction paper
different-colored tempera paints
paintbrushes and glue

Directions:
1. Fold one sheet of paper in half. (H)
2. Open the paper flat and drip different colors of paint on the center of the paper.
3. Fold the paper together again and rub on the top surface.
4. Open the paper out to find a pattern. Allow the paint to dry.
5. Cut the print into a small butterfly shape. (T)
6. Repeat steps 1-4 with the other paper.
7. Cut this print into a large flower shape. (T)
8. Glue a butterfly shape to a flower shape.

Round The Campfire

Materials For Each Child:
1 sheet of 12" x 18" white construction paper
½ sheet of 9" x 12" brown construction paper
½ sheet of 9" x 12" green construction paper
small sticks and twigs or straw
red, yellow, and orange tissue paper
gold foil
glue

Directions:
1. Tear thin strips of brown and green construction paper. Arrange them in a campfire shape on a sheet of white construction paper and glue in position.
2. Glue sticks and twigs or straw on top.
3. Tear up pieces of tissue paper, not too small, and glue them above the campfire to make flames. Add a few pieces of gold foil for a glow.

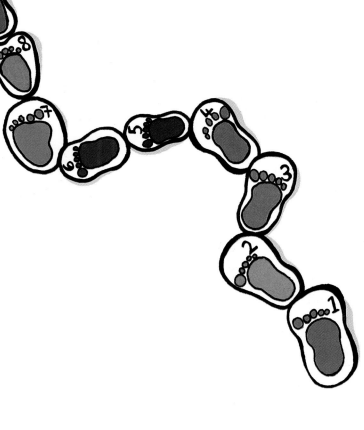

Follow The Trail

• •

Materials For Each Child:
1 sheet of 8½" x 11" tagboard
cold laminating film
different-colored tempera paints in
    large, flat containers
black marker

Class Preparations:
Pour paints into flat containers. Provide
a tub of water and towels to wash up.
Have scissors ready.

Directions:
1. Put one bare foot in a container of paint,
then step on tagboard to make a footprint.
2. Allow the print to dry; then label it with
a letter or number, as shown. Ⓗ
3. Cut out the footprint and cover with
laminating film. Ⓣ
4. Lay out the class footprints in a trail. Ⓗ
5. Step on top of the prints to follow the
letters or numbers.

Mad Hatter Party

• •

Materials For Each Child:
1 paper grocery bag
bits and pieces, such as corks, sponge, paper
    curls, and aluminum-foil balls
glue

Class Preparations:
For each child, make a 3" slit in each corner
of the grocery bag.

Directions:
1. Fold up the flaps to make the hat brim,
as shown.
2. Glue on bits and pieces to decorate your hat.

115

Summer Bonnet

. . . .

Materials For Each Child:
8 green tissue-paper leaf cutouts
1 paper plate, 10" in diameter
tissue paper in bright colors
shredded paper
elastic
glue

Class Preparations:
Use the leaf pattern on page 73 to cut about eight tissue-paper leaves for each child. Have a hole puncher ready.

Directions:
1. Crumple up pieces of colored tissue paper. Glue them with the leaves and shredded paper to the bottom of the paper plate.
2. Use a hole puncher to make holes in opposite sides of the hat and thread elastic through to hold the hat on. Tie knots to secure the elastic. ⓣ

Carnival Hat

. . . .

Materials For Each Child:
1 paper cup
1 paper plate, 10" in diameter
2 pieces of thin ribbon, 10" in length
pieces of fabric and lace, paper curls,
   streamers, feathers, and jingle bells
glue

Class Preparations:
Have your class collect materials to decorate the hats. Have a hole puncher ready.

Directions:
1. Glue the cup to the middle of the plate to make a hat with a brim, as shown.
2. Glue on bits and pieces to decorate it.
3. Use a hole puncher to make holes in opposite sides of the plate. Tie a knot at the end of each ribbon and thread them through the holes to tie the hat on. ⓣ

Prepare for July 4th with a patriotic quilt and colorful flags. Then begin the celebrations!

Red, White, And Blue Patchwork Quilt

Materials For Each Child:
1 square of white tagboard, 6" x 6"
red and blue tempera paints
paintbrushes

Class Preparations:
For this group project, cut a 6" x 6" square of tagboard for each child.

Directions:
1. Make a design or picture on the tagboard using red and blue tempera paints.
2. Allow to dry.
3. When the patches are finished, arrange them all in a pattern on a bulletin board to make a quilt. Ⓗ

Flags

Materials For Each Child:
1/2 sheet of 9" x 12" construction paper
1 dowel, 12" in length
tempera paints, fine-tip markers,
  or gummed-paper shapes
paintbrushes

Class Preparations:
Cut a 9" x 6" construction-paper flag for each child. You can also make triangular flags or square flags, if desired.

Directions:
1. Make a design on one side of the flag, using paints, markers, or gummed-paper shapes. Allow to dry.
2. Fold over about 1" on one side of the flag. Glue this flap over the dowel, as shown. Ⓗ

117

Streamers
• • • • • • • • • • • • • •

Materials For Each Child:
4 colored crepe-paper strips
1 pipe cleaner
1 straw
glue

Class Preparations:
Cut a class supply of crepe-paper strips,
each measuring about 1/2" x 41/2".

Directions:
1. Bend the pipe cleaner in half and push
both ends into the end of the straw, leaving
a loop big enough to push a finger through.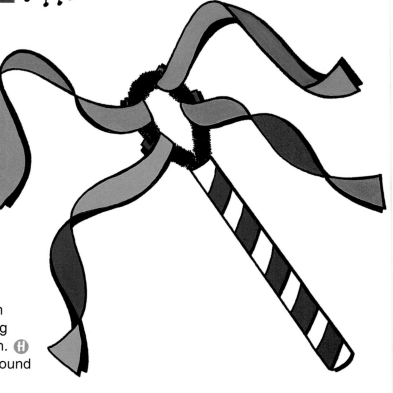
2. Fold one end of a crepe-paper strip around
the pipe cleaner loop and glue it in place.
3. Repeat with three more strips.

Patriotic Mobile
• •

Materials For Each Child:
4 white construction-paper star cutouts
2 red and 2 blue crepe-paper strips
1 metal coat hanger
glue

Class Preparations:
Use the pattern on page 45 to cut four white
stars for each child. Cut two red and two blue
crepe-paper strips, measuring 2" x 24".

Directions:
1. Fold each paper strip in half and put
a blob of glue in the fold.
2. Hang the strips over the coat hanger,
as shown, and press the glued fold firmly.
3. Glue a white star to each strip.
4. Hang up the mobile.

Give your Independence Day party a lift with a colorful rocket display along the classroom windowsill.

Blast Off!

. . . .

Materials For Each Child:
1 colored tagboard triangle cutout
1 cardboard tube
1 craft stick
aluminum foil
shredded yellow and red construction paper
glue and modeling clay

Class Preparations:
Use the pattern below to cut a tagboard triangle for each child. Have a stapler ready.

Directions:
1. Wrap aluminum foil around the cardboard tube and tuck in the ends.
2. Cut two 1" slits on opposite sides of the top of the tube. ⓣ
3. Slot the triangle into the two slits.
4. Staple shredded paper inside the other end of the rocket. ⓣ
5. Dip the end of the craft stick in glue and press to one side inside the rocket. Lay the rocket on its side and leave to dry.
6. Push the craft stick into a piece of modeling clay to display the rocket.

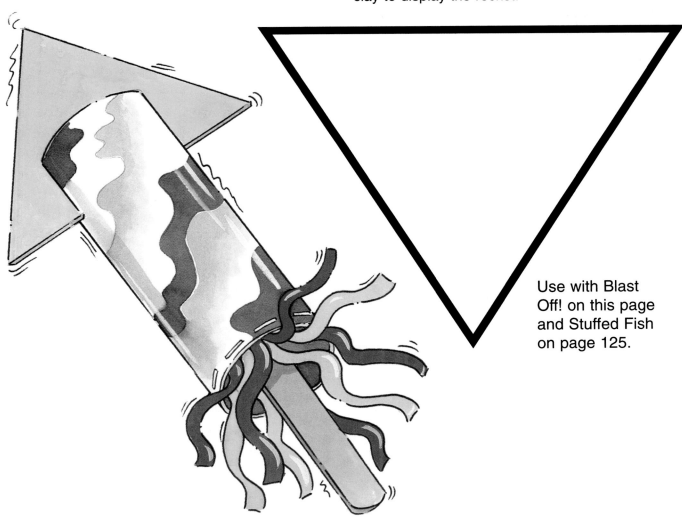

Use with Blast Off! on this page and Stuffed Fish on page 125.

119

Space Creatures

Materials For Each Child:
1 container, such as a yogurt cup, cardboard
    tube, paper cup, or dish-detergent bottle
junk items, such as pipe cleaners, paper
    scraps, wiggle eyes, corks, plastic wrap,
    aluminum foil, and string
tempera paints, paintbrushes and glue

Class Preparations:
Have your class make a collection of junk.
Wrap and glue construction paper around
plastic containers such as yogurt cups.

Directions:
1. Glue pipe cleaners, plastic wrap, aluminum
foil, and other junk to your container to create
your space creature; then allow it to dry.
2. Finish off the space creature by painting it.

Jellyfish

Materials For Each Child:
1/2 paper plate, 7" in diameter
strips of clear plastic wrap
tissue-paper scraps
long strips of crepe paper
glue

Class Preparations:
Cut the paper plates in half and give each child
half a plate. Cut the crepe paper into long strips.
Cut strips of clear plastic wrap. Have string and
tape ready.

Directions:
1. Decorate the underside of half a paper
plate by gluing on tissue paper and strips
of plastic wrap.
2. Glue crepe-paper tentacles to the straight
edge of the plate on the other side, so that
they dangle down.
3. Tape a piece of string to the middle of the
jellyfish's curved edge to hang it up. 🅣

Your youngsters will be fanatical about fish with these watery projects. Glug!

Swimming Around

Materials For Each Child:
1 sheet of 9" x 12" white construction paper
$1/2$ carrot
1 straw
very runny blue tempera paint in a container slightly larger than the construction paper
tempera paints in different colors
black fine-tip markers

Class Preparations:
Mix some very runny tempera paint with a little dish detergent in a container.
Cut carrots in half on a diagonal.

Directions:
1. Blow down the straw to make bubbles in the paint, then gently place the sheet of paper on top. Lift it off carefully, then allow to dry. 🄷
2. Dip half a carrot into paint and use it to print fish bodies on the paper. Repeat with other colors.
3. Allow to dry; then use markers to add a tail, mouth, and eyes.

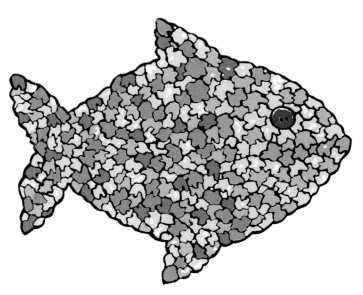

Fantastic Fish

Materials For Each Child:
1 construction-paper fish cutout
tissue paper in different colors
button and glue

Class Preparations:
Use the pattern on page 122 to cut out a fish from construction paper for each child.

Directions:
1. Spread glue on a section of the fish.
2. Crumple up balls of different-colored tissue paper and stick them on.
3. Continue until the whole fish is covered.
4. Glue on a button for an eye.

Use with Fantastic Fish
on page 121.

Hanging Fish

Materials For Each Child:
2 construction-paper fins
1 construction-paper tail
1 paper plate, 7" in diameter
aluminum-foil scraps
tempera paints and paintbrushes
glue

Class Preparations:
Use the patterns below to cut out two fins and a tail from construction paper for each child. Cut out a triangle from one side of the paper plate to make a mouth. Have a hole puncher and lengths of yarn ready.

Directions:
1. With the mouth positioned on one side, glue fins to the top and bottom of the paper plate to make a fish. Glue the tail to the back of the fish.
2. Paint the fish and add an eye. Allow to dry.
3. Glue on scales made from scraps of aluminum foil. Allow the glue to dry.
4. Use a hole puncher to make a hole in the top fin. Thread yarn through to hang the fish. Ⓣ

123

Underwater

· · · · · · · · · · · · · · · · · ·

Materials For Each Child:

1 Styrofoam® tray
1 piece of blue construction paper,
  large enough to line the tray
several construction-paper fish
  cutouts in various colors
Sticky Tac® and clear plastic wrap
crayons or colored markers and glue

Class Preparations:

Use the patterns below to cut several fish
shapes from construction paper for each child.
Cut a piece of blue construction paper large
enough to line each child's tray.

Directions:

1. Cover the inside of the tray with glue, then
stick down a piece of blue paper to line it.
2. Use crayons or colored markers to decorate
the fish shapes.
3. Using small balls of Sticky Tac®, attach the
fish shapes to the bottom.
4. Cover the top of the tray with clear plastic
wrap to give the effect of the surface of a pond. Ⓗ

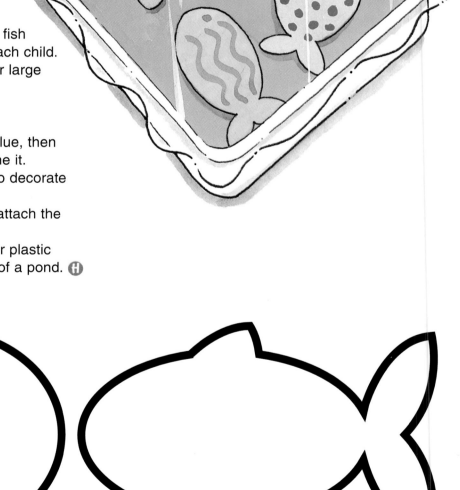

Octopus Hanger

Materials For Each Child:
1 metal coat hanger pulled into a diamond shape
1 sheet of tissue paper cut into a diamond shape
2 small white construction-paper circles
8 crepe-paper strips, 12" long
black marker and glue

Class Preparations:
Pull each coat hanger into a diamond shape.
Using the coat hanger as a template, cut a
diamond of tissue paper large enough for the
edges to fold over the hanger. Use a jar lid to cut
out two white paper circles for each child. Tear
or cut crepe paper into strips about 12" long.
Have tape and string ready.

Directions:
1. Fold the edges of the tissue-paper diamond
over the coat hanger and tape them down.
2. Glue the paper circles to one side of the
tissue paper to make eyes. Use a black marker
to add pupils and eyelashes.
3. Tape one end of each crepe-paper strip
to the bottom half of the octopus' body.
4. Use string to hang the octopus up. ⓣ

Stuffed Fish

Materials For Each Child:
4 colored construction-paper fins
2 white construction-paper eyes
1 brown paper lunch bag
newspaper and pieces of sponge
tempera paint in shallow trays
black marker and glue

Class Preparations:
Use the template on page 119 to cut four fins
from colored construction paper. Cut curves in
two of them. Use a jar lid to cut two white paper
eyes for each child. Have string ready.

Directions:
1. Sponge paint scales onto one side of a
paper bag. Allow to dry, then sponge paint the
other side. Allow this side to dry, too.
2. Stuff the bag with crumpled newspaper.
3. Tie string around the open end of the bag
to make a tail. ⓣ
4. Glue on eyes and fins, with the curved fins
on the top and bottom. Add pupils with a marker.

summer

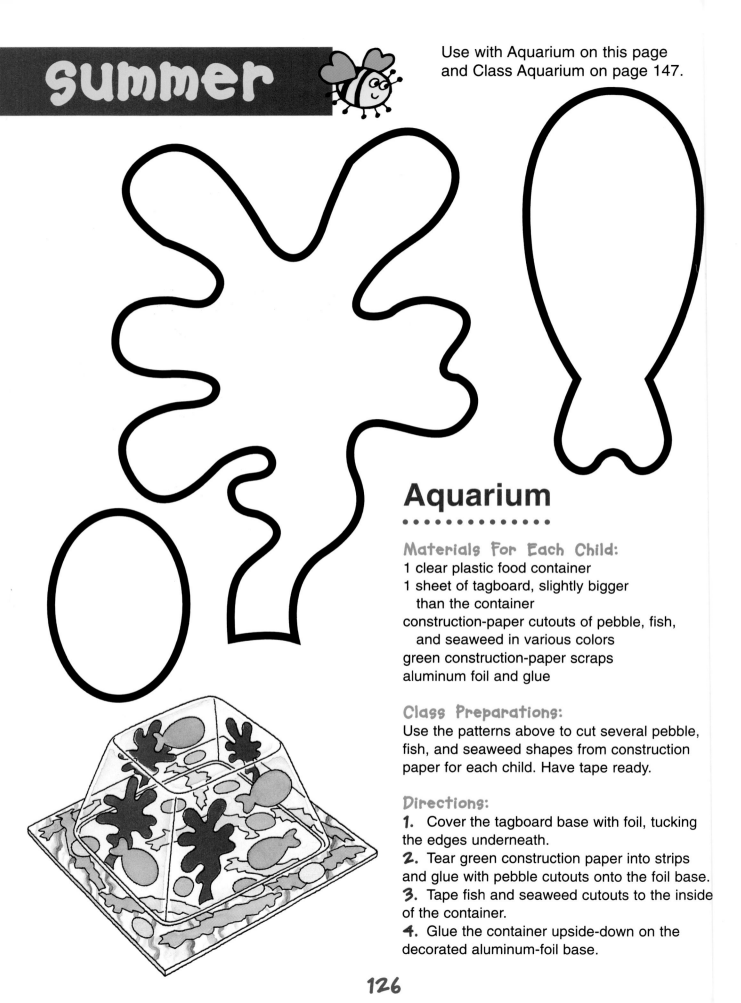

Aquarium

Materials For Each Child:
1 clear plastic food container
1 sheet of tagboard, slightly bigger
  than the container
construction-paper cutouts of pebble, fish,
  and seaweed in various colors
green construction-paper scraps
aluminum foil and glue

Class Preparations:
Use the patterns above to cut several pebble, fish, and seaweed shapes from construction paper for each child. Have tape ready.

Directions:
1. Cover the tagboard base with foil, tucking the edges underneath.
2. Tear green construction paper into strips and glue with pebble cutouts onto the foil base.
3. Tape fish and seaweed cutouts to the inside of the container.
4. Glue the container upside-down on the decorated aluminum-foil base.

Sparkly Starfish

Materials For Each Child:
1 orange construction-paper starfish cutout
1 sheet of 8½" x 11" tagboard
dry brown lentils
sequins
glue and brush

Class Preparations:
Use the pattern below to cut out a starfish from orange construction paper for each child.

Directions:
1. Glue the starfish cutout on the tagboard background.
2. Spread glue onto the rest of the tagboard and sprinkle on dry lentils.
3. Decorate the starfish with sequins to make it sparkle.

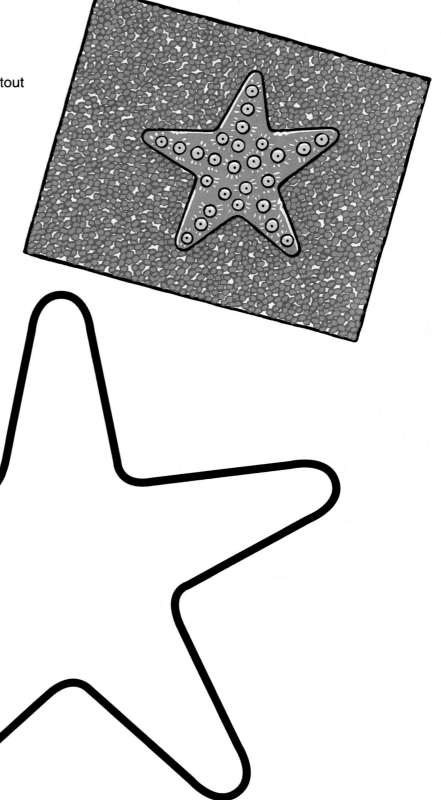

Sand and shells add an interesting texture to art projects with a summer holiday theme. Try these ideas.

Build A Sandcastle

Materials For Each Child:
1 sandpaper sandcastle cutout
1 white construction-paper flag cutout
1 sheet of 9" x 12" blue construction paper
shells or shell-shaped pasta
toothpick
yellow tissue-paper scraps
colored markers and glue

Class Preparations:
Use the patterns on the opposite page to cut a sandcastle shape from sandpaper and a white construction-paper flag for each child. Have tape ready.

Directions:
1. Glue the sandpaper castle on a sheet of blue construction paper.
2. Glue shells or pasta shells on the sandcastle.
3. Use markers to decorate the paper flag and tape the flag to a toothpick along the flag's short side. Glue the toothpick to the top of the sandcastle. ⓗ
4. Crumple up pieces of yellow tissue paper and glue them around the bottom of the sandcastle.

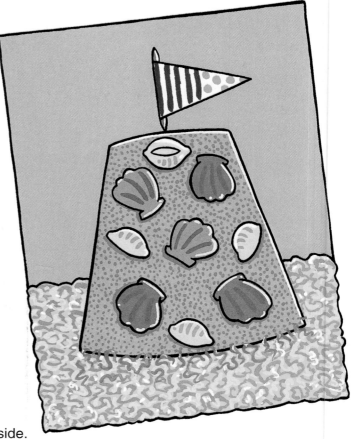

Sand Pictures

Materials For Each Child:
1 sheet of 9" x 12" posterboard
shells, sticks, and pebbles
sand and glue

Class Preparations:
Have a hot-glue gun ready.

Directions:
1. Use a hot-glue gun to glue shells, sticks, and pebbles onto the posterboard. ⓣ
2. Spread glue around the shapes.
3. Sprinkle sand on top of the glue.
4. Allow to dry; then shake loose sand off.

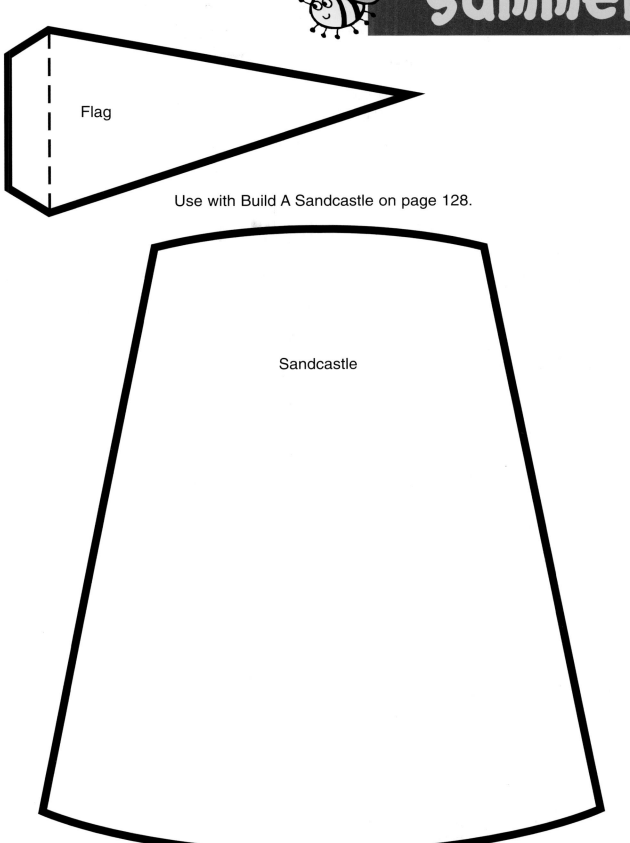

Flag

Use with Build A Sandcastle on page 128.

Sandcastle

Beach Art

. . . .

Materials For Each Child:
1 sheet of 12" x 18" posterboard
small shells, twigs, and pebbles
tempera paints in various colors, mixed
   with play sand
paintbrushes

Class Preparations:
Pour white play sand into tubs of tempera
paint and mix together.

Directions:
1. Use the thick sand and paint mix to paint
a summer scene onto a sheet of posterboard.
2. Press shells, twigs, and pebbles on the
picture before the paint dries.

Palm Tree

. . . .

Materials For Each Child:
1 cardboard tube
1 piece of green construction paper, about 4"
   taller than the tube with a fringe cut
unsalted peanuts or hazelnuts in the shell
colored markers or tempera paints
paintbrushes and glue

Class Preparations:
Cut a fringe approximately 4" long on one side
of each child's sheet of green construction paper.

Directions:
1. Use markers or paints to decorate the tube to
look like the trunk of a coconut tree.
2. Roll the green construction paper up tightly
and push into the tube so the fringe sticks out
of the tube. 🅣
3. Curl the paper back to look like palm fronds.
4. Glue nuts onto the top of the trunk to look
like coconuts.

Sundae Surprise

Materials For Each Child:
1 construction-paper sundae-glass cutout
a selection of construction-paper ice-cream
  scoop, fruit, nut, and sauce cutouts
1/2 flexible drinking straw
colored markers and glue

Class Preparations:
Duplicate the patterns on page 132 onto white
construction paper and cut out the shapes.
Provide each child with a sundae-glass cutout
and several paper ice-cream scoops, fruits,
nuts, and sauce layers. Cut straws in half
and give each child the flexible half.
Have scissors ready.

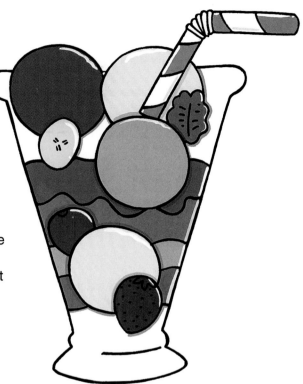

Directions:
1. Use markers to color the paper sundae
glass and the paper shapes to make your
favorite sundae ingredients, such as vanilla
or strawberry ice cream, cherries, nuts, and
layers of chocolate or caramel sauce.
2. Glue on the paper shapes to "fill the glass".
3. Trim any paper shapes that go over the
edge of the glass. ⓣ
4. Finish off by bending your
straw and sticking it in
the sundae!

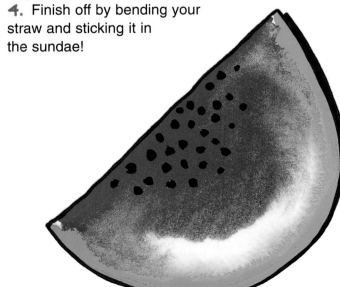

Watermelon

Materials For Each Child:
1/2 coffee filter
green, red, and black tempera paints
paintbrushes
water

Class Preparations:
Fold coffee filters in half and cut off the
scalloped edge. Cut in half and give each
child a semicircle.

Directions:
1. Dip one edge of the filter in water until
the filter is damp all over but not dripping.
2. Paint the edge of the filter green for
the melon rind.
3. Paint the center of the melon red,
allowing the colors to blend together.
4. Allow to dry; then paint on black seeds.

Use with Sundae Surprise on page 131.

anytime

These accessories will add a sparkle to role-playing activities.

Party Mask

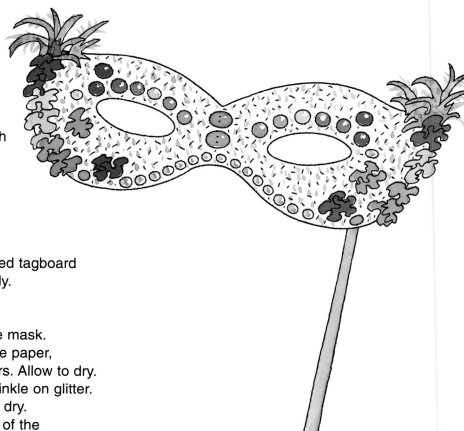

Materials For Each Child:
1 tagboard mask cutout
1 piece of dowel, 8" in length
various materials for decoration such
    as tissue paper, sequins, beads,
    buttons, and feathers
glitter
glue

Class Preparations:
Use the pattern below to cut a colored tagboard
mask for each child. Have tape ready.

Directions:
1. Spread glue over one side of the mask.
2. Decorate with crumpled-up tissue paper,
sequins, beads, buttons, and feathers. Allow to dry.
3. Spread glue in the gaps and sprinkle on glitter.
Shake off excess glitter and allow to dry.
4. Tape the dowel stick to the back of the
mask at one side, so you can hold the mask
up to your face. **H**

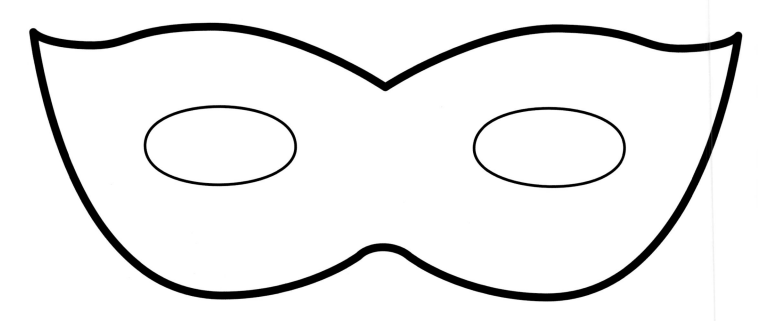

Treasure Box

Materials For Each Child:
1 small cardboard box with a lid
various materials for decoration
such as shells, dry pasta, beads,
and glitter
gold tempera paint and paintbrush
glue

Class Preparations:
Find an empty cardboard box with
a lid for each child.

Directions:
1. Glue a few pieces of pasta on the sides
of the box and on its lid. Allow to dry.
2. Brush gold paint all over the box and
pasta decorations. Allow to dry.
3. Glue shells, beads and glitter on the box
to fill the gaps.
4. Use your box for storing secret treasures.

Queen's Crown

Materials For Each Child:
1 tagboard semicircle, 14" in diameter
aluminum foil
strips of colored crepe paper, 8" in length
jellybeans and glue

Class Preparations:
Use a pin and string to draw and cut a 14" circle
from tagboard (see page 5). Cut the circle in half
and provide each child with one semicircle. Cut
crepe paper into 8" streamers. Have tape ready.

Directions:
1. Spread glue on the semicircle and cover with
aluminum foil. 🖐
2. Tape the straight edges of the semicircle
together to make a cone. 🖐
3. Decorate by gluing on jellybeans for jewels.
4. Tape the streamers to the top of the crown.

Magic Wand

• • • • • • • • • • • • • • • • • •

Materials For Each Child:
1 tagboard star cutout
glitter, sequins, or beads
1 piece of dowel, 8" in length
aluminum or gold foil
gold or silver paint
paintbrush
glue

Class Preparations:
Use the pattern on page 45 to cut a
tagboard star for each child. Have tape ready.

Directions:
1. Paint the star gold or silver on both
sides and allow to dry.
2. Glue on glitter, sequins, or beads.
3. Wind foil around the dowel and
tape at the top and bottom.
4. Tape the star onto the dowel.

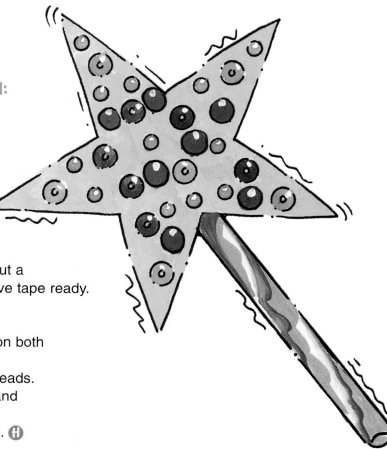

King's Crown

• • • • • • • • • • • • • • • • • •

Materials For Each Child:
1 colored construction-paper crown cutout
Lifesavers®
glue

Class Preparations:
For each child, fold a piece of 18" x 6"
construction paper in half widthwise and
cut zigzags along the top, as shown.
Have tape ready.

Directions:
1. Decorate the paper by gluing on Lifesavers®
for jewels. Allow to dry.
2. Tape the paper into a crown to fit.

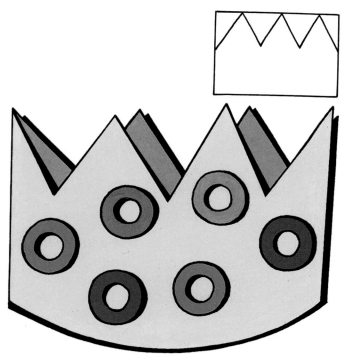

Dandy Dinosaur Crayon Holder

Materials For Each Child:
self-hardening modeling clay about the size
   of a tennis ball, or a 4 oz. pack of Crayola®
   Model Magic® modeling compound
colored crayons
brightly-colored tempera paints
paintbrushes

Class Preparations
Show your students pictures of dinosaurs,
including a Stegosaurus. Explain that no one
knows exactly what a dinosaur looked like or
how its skin was colored.

Directions
1. Roll two-thirds of the modeling clay into a
ball to form the dinosaur's body. Pinch a point to
form the head; then roll the other end into a
longer point to make the tail, as shown (A). ⊕
2. Divide the remainder of the modeling clay
into four equal parts and roll each piece into a
fat sausage shape. Attach to the body to make
legs. Smooth the joins (B). ⊕
3. Push the blunt end of a crayon firmly into the
dinosaur's back, slightly to one side of the
center. Wiggle it to make the hole slightly
wider than the crayon (C). Repeat this
step to make eight holes over the
dinosaur's back. Remove the
crayon; then allow the modeling
clay to harden.

4. Paint your dinosaur bright colors. You could
give it spots, stripes, swirls, or zigzags. Paint on
eyes, a mouth, and toes. Allow to dry.
5. Store your colored crayons in the holes on
the dinosaur's back. They will resemble the
plates on a Stegosaurus' back.

A

B

C

Rocking Mouse

• •

Materials For Each Child:
1 paper plate, 7" in diameter, folded in half
1 piece of yarn, 5" in length
6 pieces of yarn, 2" in length
black marker and glue

Class Preparations:
Fold a paper plate in half for each child.

Directions:
1. Use the marker to draw a nose, eye, and ear on each side of the paper plate.
2. Glue the long piece of yarn to the inside of the plate for a tail. Glue three shorter pieces to either side of the mouse for whiskers.

Squeak, Squeak!

• •

Materials For Each Child:
1 gray or pink construction-paper semicircle
2 gray or pink construction-paper circles
6 black construction-paper strips, 1" in length
1 piece of yarn, 4" in length
black fine-tip marker and glue

Class Preparations:
Use the patterns on page 40 to cut a class supply of large semicircles and smaller circles from gray or pink paper. Give each child a semicircle and 2 circles in contrasting colors. Cut narrow black strips, 1" in length, for whiskers. Have tape ready.

Directions:
1. Roll the semicircle into a cone and tape the edges together. ⒣
2. Glue on paper circles for ears, paper strips for whiskers, and string for a tail.
3. Use a marker to add dots for eyes.

138

Coconut Mice

Materials For Each Child:
coconut mixture
1 small piece of waxed paper
2 shelled almonds
3 silver candy balls
1 length of licorice

Class Preparations:
To make coconut mixture for 12 children, mix together 10 oz. of confectioner's powdered sugar and 8 oz. of sweetened condensed milk in a mixing bowl. Stir in 7 oz. of flaked coconut. Add a few drops of red food coloring. Divide the mixture into 12 equal parts.

Directions:
1. Roll the coconut mixture into a ball. Place on a piece of waxed paper.
2. Mold one side of the ball into a point to make a nose.
3. Push in two almonds for ears.
4. Add silver balls for the nose and eyes and a length of licorice for a tail. Allow to dry overnight.

Little Nibbler

Materials For Each Child:
1/2 sheet of 9" x 12" yellow construction paper
1 gray construction-paper square, 3" x 3"
cork, round building block, or bottle top
black tempera paint in a shallow tray
fine-tip markers, short length of string, and glue

Class Preparations:
Cut sheets of 9" x 12" yellow construction paper in half diagonally to make two triangles. Cut gray paper into 3" squares. Provide each child with one yellow triangle and one gray square.

Directions:
1. To make a piece of holey cheese, print black circles on the yellow paper triangle using a cork, round building block, or bottle top dipped in paint.
2. Fold the gray square in half diagonally to make a triangular mouse. (H)
3. Use markers to add eyes, a nose, and a mouth to each side of the mouse.
4. Glue on a string tail.
5. Place the mouse on top of the cheese.

Use these food and drink activities to encourage the children to explore different flavors and tastes.

Lemonade Smiles!

Materials For Each Child:
1 red construction-paper mouth cutout
1 white construction-paper teeth cutout
1 straw
glass of lemonade
black marker
glue

Class Preparations:
Use the patterns below to cut out a red paper mouth and white teeth for each child. Prepare lemonade together. Have a hole puncher ready.

Directions:
1. Glue the white teeth on top of the red mouth.
2. Draw on teeth with a black marker.
3. Use a hole puncher to punch a hole in the middle of the teeth; then insert a straw through it. **T**
4. Place the straw in a glass of lemonade, and drink.

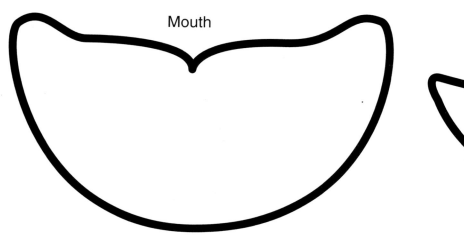

Mouth

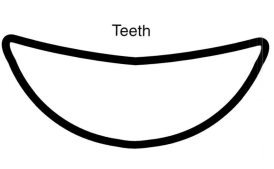

Teeth

Pick Up A Pizza

Materials For Each Child:
9 colored construction-paper pizza
   topping cutouts (mushroom, pepper,
   and pepperoni)
several yellow construction-paper strips,
   about 3" in length
1 empty pizza box
thick red tempera paint and paintbrush
pencil
glue in a squeeze bottle

Class Preparations:
Use the patterns below to cut out about
9 pizza toppings for each child from colored
construction paper. Cut yellow paper in thin strips.

Directions:
1. Draw a big, round pizza shape inside the box.
2. Paint the shape with thick red paint to look
like tomato sauce. Allow to dry.
3. Glue your favorite toppings on the pizza.
4. Squeeze lines of glue over your pizza.
Sprinkle on the yellow strips for cheese!

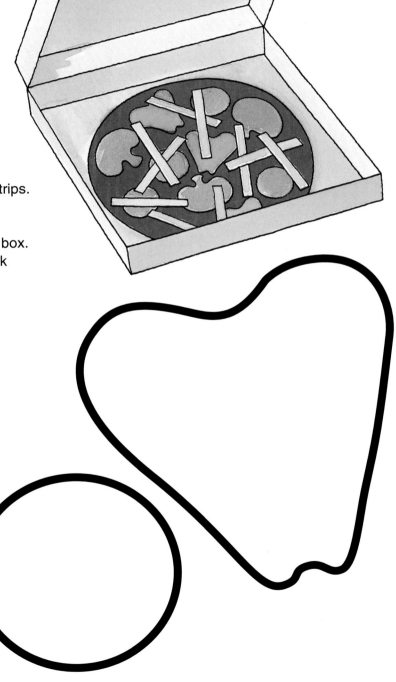

anytime

What's For Breakfast?

Materials For Each Child:
1 sheet of 15" x 10" posterboard
1 piece of 17" x 12" gingham fabric
 or wrapping paper
1 paper plate, 7" in diameter
1 paper bowl, 7" in diameter
magazines and food cartons
plastic knife, fork, and spoon
glue

Class Preparations:
Have your class collect pictures of
breakfast foods from magazines and
food cartons.

Directions:
1. Glue the fabric or wrapping paper on the
posterboard, gluing the edges underneath to
make a tablecloth.
2. Glue the paper plate and bowl onto the
tablecloth background.
3. Fill the dishes by gluing on pictures
of your favorite breakfast foods.
4. Glue a plastic knife, fork, and spoon
to your artwork.

Wheels Go Round

Materials For Each Child:
1 tagboard bus cutout
2 tagboard wheel cutouts
2 brass fasteners
tempera paints and paintbrushes

Class Preparations:
For each child, duplicate the patterns on the
opposite page onto tagboard and cut out the
shapes. Use a hole puncher to make a hole
in the wheels and bus, where marked by
small crossed circles.

Directions:
1. Paint the bus and the wheels in your
favorite colors. Allow to dry.
2. Attach the wheels loosely with brass fasteners
so that they turn. **H**

Here are some ideas to get things moving when you want projects for a transportation theme.

Use with Wheels Go Round on page 142.

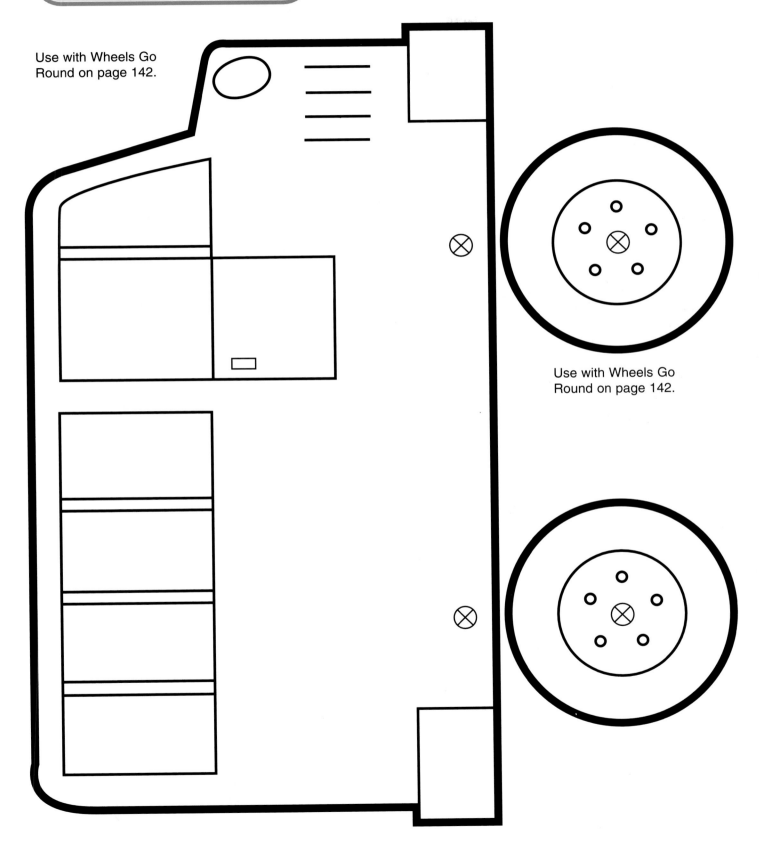

Use with Wheels Go Round on page 142.

143

Road Sense

. . . .

Materials For Each Child:
1 large sheet of bulletin-board paper
small cartons and cardboard tubes
toy cars, trucks, and buses
tempera paints
paintbrushes and glue

Class Preparations:
Have children collect small cartons
and cardboard tubes, and bring
toy vehicles into class.

Directions:
1. Paint the tubes and cartons to look like
buildings. Allow to dry.
2. Paint roads on the paper. Add a park with a
lake, or a railroad. Allow to dry overnight. ⊕
3. Glue the buildings to the base.
4. Now you're ready to drive toy cars, trucks,
and buses along the roads.

Balloon Ride

. . . .

Materials For Each Child:
1 tagboard square, 3" x 3", and 1 tagboard circle
2 ribbons, about 6" in length
1 school photo
1 craft stick
tempera paint
paintbrush

Class Preparations:
For each child, cut a 3" x 3" tagboard square and
use the pattern on page 73 to cut a tagboard
circle. Use a hole puncher to punch holes in
each shape, as shown. Have tape ready.

Directions:
1. Decorate the balloon and basket with paint.
Allow to dry.
2. Thread ribbon through the holes to attach
the balloon to the basket. Tape at the back. ⊕
3. Tape your school photo to the craft stick.
4. Tape the craft stick behind the basket so
you are ready for a balloon ride! ⊕

144

Look—Up In The Sky!

Materials For Each Child:
colored construction-paper cutouts of
   2 birds, 1 airplane, 1 kite, and 2 kite tails
1 sheet of 9" x 12" blue construction paper
small, round sponge
white tempera paint in a shallow container
glue

Class Preparations:
Duplicate the patterns below onto
different-colored construction paper
and cut out. Give each child cutouts
in a selection of colors.

Directions:
1. Use the sponge to print white clouds
on the blue paper sky.
2. Allow to dry.
3. Glue the paper cutouts on the sky.

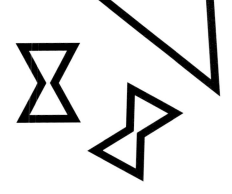

145

Sailing On The Waves

Materials For Each Child:
1 tagboard boat cutout
1 sheet of 9" x 12" construction paper
1 craft stick
sponge
tempera paints in bright colors,
   including white
blue tempera paint in a shallow container
paintbrushes
glue

Class Preparations:
Use the pattern below to cut a
tagboard boat for each child.
Have a craft knife ready.

Directions:
1. Paint the boat and allow to dry.
2. Glue the craft stick to the back of the boat.
3. Use the sponge to print blue sea on the
bottom half of the paper.
4. Use a paintbrush to add white tips to the
waves. Allow to dry.
5. Use a craft knife to cut an 8" slit in the
paper, below the waves. ⓣ
6. Poke the craft stick through the slit, and
move it about to sail your boat on the sea.

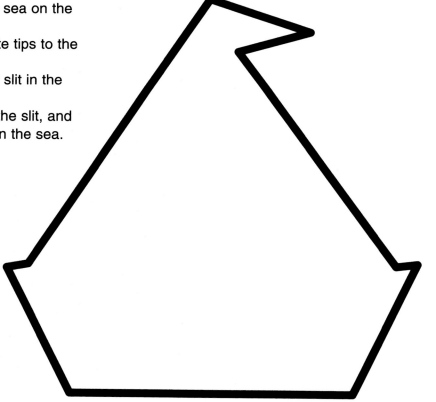

Tug Boat

Materials For Each Child:
1 large and 1 small cereal box
cork
tempera paints
paintbrush
glue

Class Preparations:
Collect one small and one large
cereal box for each child. Cut one side
from the large box as shown.

Directions:
1. Paint the large cereal box and allow to dry.
2. Paint the small cereal box to make the tug's
cabin, with windows on the sides. Allow to dry.
3. Glue the small cereal box inside the base
of the larger cereal box.
4. Glue on a cork for a smokestack.

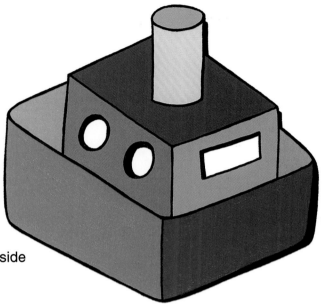

Class Aquarium

Materials For Each Child:
1 tagboard fish
1 cardboard carton or cereal box, to share
sand and pebbles
tempera paints and paintbrushes
short length of thread

Class Preparations:
For this group project, use the pattern on page
126 to cut a tagboard fish for each child. Cut out
one side of the carton, leaving a 3" frame all the
way around. Have tape and a sheet of light blue
cellophane or clear plastic wrap ready.

Directions:
1. Paint your fish on both sides. Allow to dry.
2. Help put sand and pebbles in the bottom of
the carton to make an aquarium. (H)
3. Tape a length of thread to the fish; then
tape it to the inside top of the aquarium.
4. Open the back of the box and tape a sheet of
light blue cellophane or clear plastic wrap across
the inside of the frame. Reseal the box. (T)

147

Put a bit of animal magic into your classroom! These pig ideas will fit in with projects on farming.

Piggy Magnet

Materials For Each Child:
cornstarch clay
self-adhesive magnetic strip
pink and black tempera paints
paintbrushes

Class Preparations:
Make up a batch of cornstarch clay
(see page 5).

Directions:
1. Use the clay to mold a pig's face with
ears and a snout. Allow to dry overnight. **(H)**
2. Paint the face pink and add black
eyes and nostrils. Allow to dry.
3. Attach a magnetic strip to the back
of the pig's face.

Pig Mosaic

Materials For Each Child:
1 sheet of 9" x 12" white construction paper,
  with pig outline
magazines
black marker
glue

Class Preparations:
Duplicate the pattern on the opposite page
on a sheet of white construction paper for
each child.

Directions:
1. Look through magazines and tear out all the
areas colored pink, gray, or black.
2. Tear these colored areas into small pieces.
3. Glue the pieces onto the pig's body,
overlapping them slightly, until it is covered.
4. Use a black marker to draw on an eye and
two nostrils.

Use with Pig Mosaic
on page 148.

Piggy Face

· · · · · · · · · · · · · · · · ·

Materials For Each Child:
1 large and 1 small pink tagboard circle
2 pink tagboard ear cutouts
1 strip of pink construction paper, 1½" x 8"
black marker
glue

Class Preparations:
For each child, use the pattern on page 73 to cut a large tagboard circle, and the patterns on this page to cut a small tagboard circle for a snout and two tagboard ears. Cut a 1½" x 8" construction-paper strip for each child.

Directions:
1. Glue the ears in place at the top of the large circle to make the pig's face.
2. Draw two dots on the large circle for eyes.
3. Accordion-fold the paper strip and glue one end to the center of the pig's face.
4. Draw dots on the small circle for the nostrils.
5. Glue the small circle to the other end of the paper strip.

Use with Piggy Face on this page and Fine Swine on page 151.

Use with Piggy Face on this page and Fine Swine on page 151.

Fine Swine

• • • • • • • • • • • • • • •

Materials For Each Child:
1 large and 1 small paper plate
2 pink construction-paper ear cutouts
1 pink construction-paper circle
2 wiggle eyes
1 brass fastener
pink tempera paint in shallow trays
pieces of sponge
black marker and glue

Class Preparations:
For each child, use the patterns on page 150 to cut a small circle for a snout and two ears from construction paper.

Directions:
1. Sponge pink paint on the back of the paper plates; then allow to dry.
2. Poke a brass fastener through the center of the smaller plate; then loosely attach this plate near the bottom of the larger plate. ⓣ
3. Draw two ovals on the snout for nostrils.
4. Glue the snout over the brass fastener, and add ears and wiggle eyes on the smaller plate. Give it a gentle push to make your pig's head swing from side to side!

Wiggly Worm

• • • • • • • • • • • • • • • • • • •

Materials For Each Child:
1/2 sheet of 9" x 12" posterboard
1 pink pipe cleaner
green tempera paint or marker
paintbrush

Class Preparations:
Use a hole puncher to punch four holes in the posterboard, as shown.

Directions:
1. Use paint or a marker to draw grass on the posterboard.
2. Allow to dry.
3. Push the pipe cleaner in and out of the holes to make a wiggly worm.

151

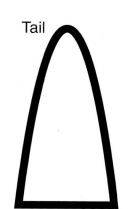

A "Turtle-rific" Pet

Materials For Each Child:
4 green construction-paper turtle feet cutouts
1 green construction-paper head cutout
1 green construction-paper tail cutout
1 paper plate, 7" in diameter
2 wiggle eyes
1 shallow box, at least 12" x 10"
shredded paper
yellow and green tempera paints
paintbrush
glue

Class Preparations:
Use the patterns on this page to cut four turtle feet, one head, and one tail from green construction paper for each child.

Directions:
1. Paint the back of the paper plate yellow; then allow to dry.
2. Paint green spots on the plate to resemble a turtle's shell.
3. Glue the straight edge of each turtle shape under the edge of the shell, as shown. 🄗
4. Glue wiggle eyes onto the turtle's head.
5. Display your turtle in a box filled with shredded paper.

Feet

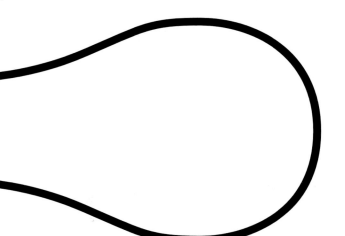

Head

Tail

Pet Snake

• • • • • • • • • • • • •

Materials For Each Child:
1 white construction-paper strip, 4" x 18"
string
tempera paints
paintbrushes
markers

Class Preparations:
For each child, cut a 4" x 18" construction-paper strip. Cut each end of the strip into a point for the head and tail. Have a hole puncher and lengths of string ready.

Directions:
1. Accordion-fold the strip of paper. ⊕
2. Paint the sections of the snake in different colors. Allow to dry.
3. Use markers or paint to add eyes.
4. Use a hole puncher to punch a hole in the snake's head and tie string through it. ⊤
5. Take your pet snake for a walk!

Crazy Snake

• • • • • • • • • • • • • • • • •

Materials For Each Child:
3 adjoining sections of an egg carton
1 red construction-paper forked tongue
2 wiggle eyes
tempera paints and paintbrushes
glue

Class Preparations:
Cut egg cartons so that each child has three adjoining sections. Cut a red forked tongue for each snake.

Directions:
1. Paint the carton with zigzags, stripes, or spots to look like a snake.
2. Allow to dry.
3. Glue on wiggle eyes and the forked tongue.

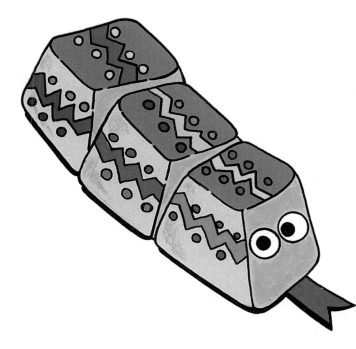

153

Caterpillar Card
• •

Materials For Each Child:
1 piece of 3" x 9" construction paper
1 straw and 1 small envelope
half a carrot
green tempera paint in a shallow tray
black fine-tip marker

Class Preparations:
Accordion-fold the construction paper into six sections for each child. Cut carrots in half.

Directions:
1. Dip the carrot in the green paint and print a circle on each section of the paper for the caterpillar's head and body.
2. Print grass along the bottom of the paper using the side of the straw.
3. Use a fine-tip marker to draw eyes, a nose, and antennae on the caterpillar's head.
4. Print a caterpillar head on an envelope and draw on eyes, a nose, and antennae.

Friendly Snake
• •

Materials For Each Child:
1 red construction-paper forked tongue
1 sheet of 9" x 12" white construction paper
small jar lid
building blocks
2 wiggle eyes
tempera paints in shallow trays
glue

Class Preparations:
Cut a red construction-paper forked tongue for each child.

Directions:
1. Use the jar lid to print overlapping circles in the shape of a snake on the paper. You could use the top of the lid to print a solid shape, or the bottom to print an outline.
2. Allow to dry.
3. Use building blocks to print colorful patterns on top of your snake; then allow to dry.
4. Glue a tongue and wiggle eyes on your snake.

Pencil Pal

Materials For Each Child:
self-hardening modeling clay in various colors
cookie cutters, to share
pencil

Class Preparations:
Use a rolling pin to roll out clay and together
cut out shapes with cookie cutters or tools.

Directions:
1. Roll a large ball of clay for the body
and a smaller one for the head. Push the
two together.
2. Use other colors of clay to add ears, eyes,
and a nose.
3. Use cut-out shapes to decorate the body.
4. Poke holes in the body using the blunt end
of a pencil. Make sure the holes are slightly
bigger than your pencil.
5. Remove the pencil and allow the clay to
harden; then use your pencil pal to store
colored pencils.

"Achoo" Bug

Materials For Each Child:
1 small tagboard circle, 2" in diameter
1 box of tissues
2 wiggle eyes
1 pipe cleaner cut in half
construction-paper shapes
tempera paint and paintbrush
black marker and glue

Class Preparations:
Use a jar lid to draw and cut out a 2" tagboard
circle for each child. Cut assorted construction-
paper shapes and cut the pipe cleaners in half.

Directions:
1. Paint the tissue box and allow to dry; then
decorate the box with cut-out paper shapes.
2. Glue wiggle eyes on the tagboard circle
and draw on a mouth to make a head. ⒣
3. Twist the pipe cleaners and glue to the
back of the head for antennae.
4. Glue the head on a short end of the box.

Here are some creative gift wrap ideas. They'll make the gift projects in this book extra special.

Forkupine

Materials For Each Child:
1 sheet of 9" x 12" construction paper
plastic fork
different-colored tempera paints
  in shallow dishes
black marker and pencil

Class Preparations:
Pour a thin layer of paint into
shallow dishes.

Directions:
1. Draw an oval on your paper.
2. Dip a plastic fork into the paint and press it down repeatedly on the paper to fill the oval. Print some fork patterns going over the edge of the oval. Allow to dry.
3. Use a marker to add a head, nose, mouth, and eye.

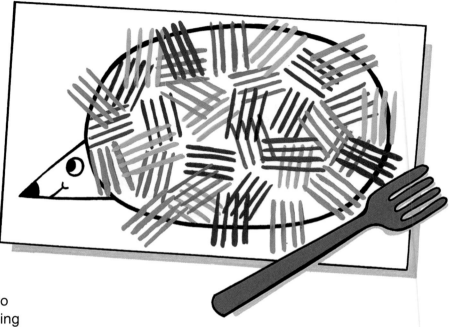

Festive Paper

Materials For Each Child:
1 sheet of 12" x 18" newsprint
tennis balls, to share
different-colored, thin tempera paints
  in shallow containers

Class Preparations:
Cover the floor with newspaper.

Directions:
1. Dip a tennis ball in the paint.
2. Drop the ball onto the paper to make a splashy print.
3. Repeat with different colors until the paper is covered. Allow to dry.
4. Hang on a clothesline or use to wrap gifts.

Bubble Printing

Materials For Each Child:
1 sheet of 9" x 12" construction paper
3 different-colored tempera paints mixed
   with liquid dish detergent in plastic
   containers larger than 9" x 12", to share
1 straw

Class Preparations:
Pour liquid dish detergent into each of three
containers. Add a different color of paint and
a little water to each.

Directions:
1. Dip the end of a straw into one of the
containers. Blow to make bubbles, being
careful not to drink the liquid by mistake.
2. Lay the paper gently on top of the bubbles.
3. Lift off the paper to see the bubble print.
4. Hang up the print to dry. (T)

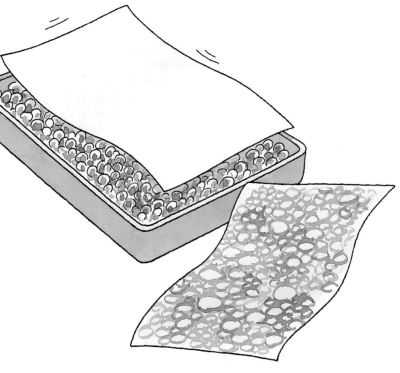

Roller Printing

Materials For Each Child:
1 sheet of 9" x 12" construction paper
printing tubes, to share
1 piece of dowel, longer than tubes
tempera paints on cookie sheets, to share

Class Preparations:
Make printing tubes by winding string around
some tubes several times and securing the ends.
Glue pieces of sponge to other tubes. Put a
small amount of paint on each cookie sheet.

Directions:
1. Put the dowel in the printing tube and use it
as a handle when you roll the tubes in the paint.
2. Roll a tube in paint and then over a sheet of
construction paper to make a pattern.
3. Repeat with a different color and tube; then
allow to dry.
4. Use the paper for wrapping gifts.

Sand Squiggles

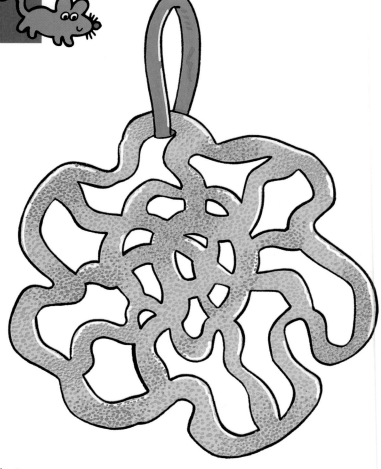

Materials For Each Child:
1 square of waxed paper, 6" x 6"
1 piece of narrow ribbon, 8" in length
colored sand in different colors
glue in a squeeze container

Class Preparations:
Practice this craft the week before to get the glue lines thick enough to peel.

Directions:
1. Squeeze a glue design onto waxed paper, making sure that all the glue lines are thick and connected.
2. Sprinkle colored sand on the design.
3. Allow to dry for a week.
4. When it is completely dry, gently peel the waxed paper from the glue design.
5. Tie a loop of ribbon on the design so that it can be hung from a window, ceiling, or wall. Ⓣ

Quick–And–Easy Stencil Picture

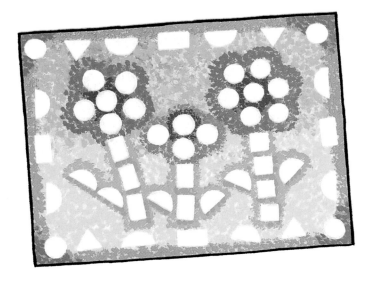

Materials For Each Child:
1 sheet of 9" x 12" waxed paper
peelable stickers
tempera paints in shallow containers
small sponges

Directions:
1. Stick peelable stickers onto the waxed paper to make a picture or pattern.
2. Use the sponges to dab paint all over the paper. Use a different sponge for each color.
3. Allow to dry.
4. Peel stickers off to reveal the picture or pattern.

Sun Shimmers

Materials For Each Child:
1 clear plastic drink-container lid
colored tissue-paper shapes
length of thin ribbon and glue

Class Preparations:
Use a hole puncher to punch a hole
near the edge of each lid. Prepare
a class supply of tissue-paper shapes.

Directions:
1. Glue tissue-paper shapes on the lid.
2. Thread ribbon through the hole.
3. Hang near the window so that the sun
can shine through. ⓣ

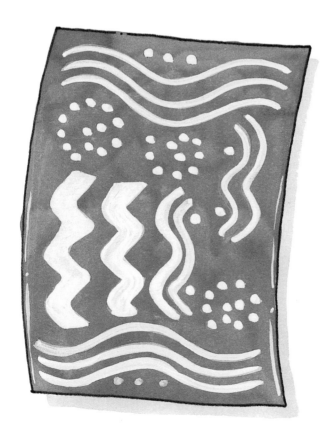

Shiny Picture

Materials For Each Child:
1 sheet of 9" x 12" construction paper
plastic fork and spoon
ruler
vinegar, sugar, and dry tempera paint mixed
  in a plastic bowl

Class Preparations:
Mix one part vinegar with two parts sugar. It is
best to use a screw-top jar and shake to mix.
Pour a small quantity into a plastic bowl and add
a little dry tempera paint. Mix with a plastic fork
to form a paste.

Directions:
1. Spoon the paste onto the paper and
spread it evenly with a ruler. Allow to dry until
it becomes slightly sticky.
2. Use the edge of the ruler and the plastic
fork to drag patterns in the paste.
3. Allow to dry until the picture is shiny.

Giraffe Height Chart

• •

Materials For Each Child
1 sheet of 9" x 12" yellow construction paper
brown tempera paint
sponge and glue

Class Preparations
Enlarge the giraffe pattern on yellow bulletin-board
paper and cut out. Use markers to add an eye,
nose, and mouth. Attach to another sheet of
bulletin-board paper, at least 4' long. Use a
marker and ruler to mark feet and inches on the
giraffe's long mane; then tape to the classroom
wall. Have twigs ready for
horns and tape ready.

Directions
1. Dip a sponge
in brown paint and
dab gently on a sheet
of yellow construction
paper. Allow
to dry.

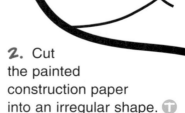

2. Cut
the painted
construction
paper
into an irregular shape. **T**
3. Glue the shape on the
giraffe's neck. **T**
4. Tape twigs on top of the
giraffe's head for horns.
5. Have a friend help you measure
your height against the giraffe. **H**